Red Storm

Vanessa Y. Reed

RoseDog✿Books
PITTSBURGH, PENNSYLVANIA 15238

RoseDog Books
585 Alpha Drive
Suite 103
Pittsburgh, PA 15238
Visit our website at *www.rosedogbookstore.com*

ISBN: 978-1-4809-7261-2
eISBN: 978-1-4809-7238-4

DEDICATION

I To my mom who have preceded her children in death, we love and miss you dearly. Mom, I wrote this book to help release the pain I carried all my life. It is in no way to bring shame to you. It is to help those who suffer in silence as I did.

TO MY SIBLINGS

In writing my memoir, I know it may cause pain to my siblings. Please know I would never cause any intentional harm to you. I truly love you all with my whole heart. To my sister Cheryl whom I've always admired, thank you for taking care of mommy. I know how close you and mom were. Please understand, I wrote this book with Gods guidance to free myself of the hurt and pain I lived with. I love you, my older only sister. To my eldest brother Darryl, I love you big brother. I always felt we were the closest amongst the four of us. You always put cash in my kids and my pockets. Thank you for fixing every repair needed in my apartments. I love and appreciate you. To my brother Steven who is a year older than I am, thank you for always protecting me. I remember when you were stabbed defending me. To this day you're still very overprotective of me. I love you brother. My brothers still introduce me to people as "their little sister". I'm honored to be the baby of the family. To my cousin Maurice, I truly love you. We grew up together because my mom raised you. You are more than my cousin, you are my big brother. To my step-father Lenny who raised me. Thank you for always being there for me. I truly love you. Last, but certainly not least: To my children, Johnny, Andrew, Shana, and Haashim, I love you all to the moon and back. Thank you for always being in my corner. As many times as I have failed you all, thank you for never failing me. I am proud of each and every one of you. As I watch my children evolve into adults, I can honestly say they are doing a great job as parents and role models to their children. Thank you for loving me. Thank you for my grandchildren Keianna, Terrance, Donte, Jerimah, and Zyaire. They bring so much joy into my life. I am truly blessed to be called "grandma". To my Nephews, Nieces and their children, I love you all so much. You all are an inspiration to me. I love the bond you all have with each other. Keep up the good work. To my Aunt Pastor Carrie, thank you for bringing me to Christ. When everyone else gave up on me you kept me lifted up. You encouraged and pushed me to do better. Thank you for never giving up on me. I love you dearly. To my Uncles, Cousins and extended family, I love you all.

TO A VERY SPECIAL FRIEND

To my best friend James McRae, thank you for always being there for me. You are truly my brother from another mother. Thank you for your words of wisdom. You have taught me so much. Thank you to your beautiful wife Laura who taught me how to have faith. I love you both.

TRUE FRIENDSHIPS NEVER DIE

To every friend who was in my life during my time of Domestic Violence, I say thank you. Thank you for never abandoning me. I am fortunate to still have those same friends in my life to this day. Thank you for the many times you helped me hide from my abuser, putting your own lives in danger. Thank you to my special sister/friend who broke her foot while helping me run for my life. Thank you to my sister/friend who use to hide me in the Laundry Mat when he would come to beat me up. Thank you to the many friends who offered me a place to stay when I had no place to go, to afraid to go home for fear he would kill me.

Laura, Leslie, Kim, Drettia, Niecy, Valerie, Wanda, Tanya, Faye, Lelet, Patrice, Mrs. Helen, Marie, Keisha, Sharevia, Sabrina, Mookie, Pearl, Anita B, and Roxanne, Thank you all for your friendship. These women have each been in my life for 35 + years. True friendships never die.

There are too may many friends to name but I LOVE YOU ALL.

To Ian and Terrence, two of the best friends a girl could ever ask for. Take care of my momma in heaven. She loved you both so much.

God Bless you all.

INTRODUCTION

I was anointed to write this book from giving my testimony at different events. On several occasions while sharing my testimony, I would notice people in the audience dabbing their eyes. I didn't realize the extent of the things I went through, until I saw the reactions of these complete strangers. When it's you going through it may not seem that relevant because it's you going through it. I remember one day sitting in bible study and a question was asked have anyone ever been through a life threatening experience. I have been through several, but I sat there wondering if I wanted to tell my business.In the room were seated about thirty men and women. The person who asked the question shared his experience and a woman followed behind him with her story. After a little contemplation my spirit said to me "share". I began to tell about the time I tried to jump out the window to escape being beat. The bible study group wasso quiet that I could hear people breathing. The women were looking at me like wow did she just share that and the men were looking at me like wow you been through that. I started laughing after telling my story. I immediately apologized to the group and explained that I didn't mean to laugh, I told them I know domestic violence is not a laughing matter but this is how I have learned to cope with my pain. The person leading the bible study said to me 'You don't owe anyone in here an apology'" he said "if that's how you've learned to deal with what you went through you keep on laughing" I felt a little better hearing this but I was still embarrassedbecause I knew everyone was looking at me. He then continued and said "The reason you didn't jump out the window is because God is going to use you" now I am almost in tears, first because I was new to going to church as an adult learning how to be a Christian. Second, I didn't see what God could have possibly seen in me to use. I had been beaten, battered and abused and felt unworthy of being loved or even loving myself. So why would God use me? I didn't know what faith was, how to have faith, how to apply faith, how to seek faith or how to believe faith even existed. I thought faith was something that you already had, not something you received as you grow in Christ. I didn't think I wanted faith because I never had a reason to have faith. I was used to living life on life terms. If something bothered me I handled it my own way which normally was a fight or lashing out. My mouth was reckless and my attitude was even worse. I didn't understand why I was so angry throughout my early years growing up. I was on a self-destructive course and I was the teacher and the student. Sounds crazy right, but that's what it was. I felt I wasn't ever going to allow anyone to hurt me again, especially a man. Men were my enemies because all my abuse and molestation came from them. So, back to my introduction as to why I wrote this book. I started talking about what I had been through in life with my church family. The more I shared the less I began to care about what people thought about my past. See, there was a time in my life when I would have never shared my past with anyone. I felt it wasn't anyone's business because all people like to do is gossip. But if you look in their closets skeletons would fall out. Also, I grew up in the era of what happens in this house stays in this house, so you didn't take the family business outside of the four walls of home. What I don't think parents took into consideration was the damage they were causing us children. We had to hold in all we were going through, all the family secrets, which became generation curses. We were stuck with carrying baggage from our childhood into our adulthood. Then they wondered why we were so messed up emotionally and mentally and can't foster healthy relationships with people. We then put a wall up and will not allow anyone to penetrate it or get close to you becauseyou are afraid they will cause more hurt and pain. Through being damaged you become defensive against people. We are now in a shell and you don't want to come out because of fear. So you come out swinging at everything and everyone. You don't know who the enemy is or who truly have your best interest at heart. The sad part to this behavior is people will avoid you because they think you are some horrible person, when you are still a child in a grown up body, who didn't really have a childhood. You were cheated out of your youth and now you are angry with the world. You feel like everyone failed you and you. You can't take the hurt out on the people who really deserve it because you love/hate them so you end up taking the pain out on everyone else. I remember when I first started giving my testimony, I would talk about domestic violence. I believed that was the most traumatic experience in my life, so that was the focus of my testimony. There were so many people still experiencing domestic violence so I didn't mind sharing. After I would tell my story women would come up to me and share their experience with domestic violence. I was shocked at some of the stories I would hear. Every story is touching and heartfelt especially as a survivor your heart goes out to someone still suffering. I began to realize that abuse isn't just physical but also verbal, mental, emotional and abuse causes stress which breaks down the bodies immune system. I never understood when I heard stress can kill you but your body reacts to being beat down emotionally. One day I was giving my testimony and before I start I always pray and ask God to speak through my vocal cords, to let my testimony be to glorify him and not myself. As I was preparing to speak I heard the voice of the Lord say speak about drug abuse. I'm like Huh!! My reaction was to look upto the ceiling and say really God, you want me to stand in front of these strangers and talk about when I use to smoke crack. Now, I was use to speaking about domestic violence and I was comfortable with sharing but this was different for me. Domestic violence is not your fault or a choice, but doing drugs is a decision you make. Most addicts make a choice to get high. I won't sit here and say someone made me do drugs, I made a conscious decision to get high. I may not have known the severity the addiction would get or even how addictive certain drugs were, but I cannot say I was forced to get high. It was the in thing to do and mostly everyone I knew was getting high in one form or another. So, I remember standing on that stage like God how do I introduce this topic to the audience and God said just be honest. I started out by telling the audience what exactly happened after I prayed. What was so ironic to me was as I looked out at my audience it was full of kids. Young kids, school aged kids and teenagers. I thought to myself wow God I now understand the importance of my testimony. I am a part of an organization called 'WE OFFER CHRIST" which is a group formed by a deeply spiritual Elder who had a vison and decided to make it a reality. We have musicians, praise dancers, singers and testimonials. We go to different States and events to perform. We were in Connecticut and I remember so well because it was my first time having talked about drug abuse. I saw my group members looking at me as this was their first time hearing me talk about being addicted to drugs. I just let the truth flow and before I knew it I was crying. I've cried before it is very emotional bringing all your past to the surface. I learned to bury my past but that is like pouring cement without first making hole. We put a top cover over an unfinished product. How am I going to cover the hole without first digging up the foundation? We have to empty out first. Wehave to pour out the dirty water of our lives and refill it with clean water. The only way we can truly heal is to accept the things we cannot change and change the things we can. Wecannot change our past but we can reshape our future. People like to throw your past in your face, like you don't know what the heck you've been through. God did not make yesterday to ever be returned. We can look forward to tomorrow, next week, next month but we will never return to yesterday. Yes, we can revisit the past to help us not want to return to the same mistakes but we shouldn't dwell in the past. After giving my testimony about drug addiction, several kids came and hugged me. I knew I had accomplished what God had set out for me to do. I never felt so touch by sharing my testimony. I was brought to tears that these children received a word in me sharing my life experience. I then realized that I have to always let the Holy Spirit lead me when I give my testimony. I could no longer do this my way because souls need to be healed. I'm now giving my testament about how God delivered me and I had my own realization, the drug abuse and domestic violence went hand and hand. Truthfully, the reason I didn't share about my drug abuse was because I was ashamed of that part of my life. Thank God he had his hands on me when I didn't even know he saw me. In those days I wasn't a Christian and wasn't thinking about Christianity. I was young and thought I was living the life, drinking, drugging, partying then being beat. I didn't understand that life had a purpose, I just thought that life was to be lived. I'm now giving my testimony from New York to South Carolina and the more I gave it the more baggage I freed from myself. Well, I'm about to give my testimony at another church, let me just say I always pray out loud for the audience to share in my prayer. I want people to know my testimony is real and for the Glory of God. I want people to know if God did it for me he can do it for them as well. God loves all of us the same. This time I am up on the platform ready to speak and God said speak about molestation. I almost fell over. I'm like God you can't really be serious. How am I supposed to stand here and talk about having survived being molested as a little girl, when I have never and I mean never talked about this, not as a child, not as a teenager and not as an adult. So I'm stuck now standing there like a lump on a log. I don't even know where or how to start. How am I going to help someone when I haven't even helped myself with this unresolved pain? One thing I have never done as a survivor of molestation, is seek help or guidance for this. I suppressed this because it was something I never wanted to face. I didn't want to open up old wounds for myself. Remember what happens here stays here.I had that mind frame that was instilled in me as a child. Thedomestic violence and drug abuse was something I could have controlled but the molestation I had no control over and I didn't want to revisit that trauma. I was a child and I could not control what I was forced to endure. I didn't know where to start so I asked God and again he said be honest. I started by telling the audience that I didn't want to testify about this but I had no choice. I gave them a brief synopsis of my domestic violence and drug history, I then in my obedience to God, talked about being a survivor of molestation. I heard the audience gasp. It was like they were saying wow domestic violence, drug addiction and molestation but I kept speaking and tried to ignore the stares I was getting. I spoke about remembering the smell of the men, the inappropriate touch of the men to my private parts, the tears I would cry and how it made me feel when my mom didn't rescue or protect me. How I wanted to tell but no one would believe me because I was always called "fast a**" or told "you're to grown". I was a child but only God can bring back events that I totally suppressed. God don't want us to live in our past but we have to heal the broken wounds, the scars, the hurt and the pain in order to move on. I am ready for the new me. My new life, my new beginning. If it took for me to write this book to have a rebirth then I am truly blessed for this opportunity. However, I won't take any credit for what God have done and is doing in my life. God put it in me to make a change. It wasn't my strength or even my decision to give my life to Christ. God picked me up, turned me around and placed my feet on solid ground. IT GETS GREATER LATER. GLORY HALLELUJAH.

Chapter 1

The Beginning

I use to wonder why me? Even as a young child I couldn't understand why I looked different, why I was teased because I looked different, why grown men felt the need to want to fondle my young undeveloped body, why no one helped me, why I felt so alone and unloved at such an early tender age in my life. I remember when I first realized I looked different having bright orange hair and all my siblings and extended family all had black hair. I remember asking my mom as a child why I look different and she told me I was special. My siblings would tell me I was adopted. I being a child didn't even know what being adopted meant so I believed them. I remember as a child my mom's boyfriends would touch my private parts when my mom was not around, at the store or visiting family or friends in our Langston Hughes Project building we lived in. My family lived in one building, my great Grandmother, grand-mother, Aunts, and cousins all lived in one building. I remember the family feuds we would have with other families. I remember my first fight. There was this family who through they ran the projects. They would start trouble with every family and a lot of people were afraid of them. Well my family wasn't. We didn't take any mess and we constantly has family brawls with them. I re-member the brother threw my sisters coat down the incinerator and my grand-mother picked him up off his feet with one hand held around this neck and dropped him to the floor. I remember the little sister always picked on me and one day were outside playing in the back of the projects and we had the concert tables with the checker board on top and she stood on top of table and there were some buckets of tar that they were using to do some repairs in the projects with, she stood on top of the table where I was standing and poured tar on hair my whole pony tail was covered in tar. I ran upstairs with all my cousins in tow and cried to my mom. I remember my whole family decided this went too far and we all went down stairs to throw down. When the elevator door opened on the first floor Kay-Kay was standing there waiting to get in the elevator and my mother and grandmother said hit her now. I was scared and didn't want to fight her but I remember the look on my momma face when she said if you don't whip her tail I am going to beat your tail right here in front of everyone. Now I was a child and I never had a fight before so I didn't know what to do. I remember just walking up to her and swinging on her and the fight was on. We fought into the elevator, out the elevator, in the hallway. I don't remember what I was doing during the fight but I do know she was crying and everybody was telling me I did a good job. I remember my cousin beating up their brother. Their family sure didn't bother us again actually we became good friends with their family but we still never trusted them. Living in Langston Hughes was horrible. Not only was it the first time I was introduced to molestation had my first fight and had to get my ponytail cut off, I also had to experience violence that no child should have had to see at such a young age. I remember someone got thrown off the roof mind you our building 335 Sutter avenue had 23 floors. Imagine someone getting thrown off the roof of a 23 story building, there was nothing left to him not even a head. People us to always fall down the elevator shaft. The elevator would come and no elevator would be there and the doors would open as though the elevator was there and if you weren't careful you would step right into the shaft. This has happened several times mainly because the elevator never had a light bulk someone would always break it or steal it and put it in their house. I remember our first fish tank, I remember our first dog and I remember that being the last time I saw my father I was about 7 years old. I remember my father had one leg. He was amputated from the knee down. I don't remember why. I don't think I was ever told why. I remember my father would bend down on his one leg and sit me on his good leg. I loved having a father and I never understood why he left one day and I never saw him again to this very day. I remember... The pain I would experience when grown men would stick their finger in my private part and then give me a dollar and threaten me not to tell or I would get a beaten. I remember thinking this was ok because they would give me my dollar afterwards so I started looking forward to getting a dollar. I would act like I was sleep when the men would come into my room to touch me. One particular man would still feel on me and then put the dollar in my panties. One day I went to my mom and showed her what I found in my panties when I woke up and I remember she took the dollar from me but never questioned where did I get the dollar from. I remember being in my bed and he would come into my room late at night he would sit on the floor on the side of my bed and slide his hand under the blanket and fondle me. I would lay there scared not making any noise because I thought I would get a beaten for being awoke so late. The fear caused me to start peeing in the bed because I was too afraid to move. I would get beat for peeing in my bed but I wasn't getting beat for having money as a child who didn't have any means of acquiring an income. I remember my siblings and cousins would tease because I wet the bed. They would say "Red head pees in the bed" which use to hurt me and make me cry. I don't think I fully understood what was happening to me being touch as a child but I did know it was not right. I remember my sister being right in the same room with me as this was happening to me. I never knew why I just didn't scream or cry out. I looking back at things now I was just a child and I really didn't know any better. As I got older it got worse to the point that I did not want to go to sleep for fear I would be touched. I became angry and began lashing out as a child. I remember in public school I was teased constantly for having what was described as orange hair. I remember the names so well 'Red headed woodpecker' 'Red head pee in the bed" 'Annie" " we albino" these names may not seem so bad as an adult but imagine you as a child and everyone and I mean everyone always teased you just because of the color of your hair. There weren't very many red headed children around so I had to endure this trauma for a long time. Not realizing my anger from being teased on a daily basis, I began to lash out and fight everyone who would tease me. So here I am a child who should be enjoying her childhood but instead I am enduring molestation and being teased. As my mom moved on with her life and got another boyfriend I thought I was now free of the touching. Not the case, to my disappointment the new boyfriend began to do the same thing to me. This time it got worse. He would stick his nasty tongue in my mouth. I remember wanting to throw up, bite his tongue, scream, but all I could do was cry you see my mom moved us in with him in his mom's house so if I made any trouble for my mom we would be put out of his mother's house.

Chapter 2

I Used to Wonder Why Me

I remember we started going to Church which was right next door to the house we were living in. That was the happiest time of my life having something to look forward to. I loved going to church as a child. I didn't know much about Church but I remember singing on the children's choir, going to Sunday school but most of all I felt protected from the creep my mom called her boyfriend. We went to Light House church of Love and Peace in East New York. I remember the giant O'Henry candy bars we would get at church and the blocks of cheese they would give out. One Sunday after service everyone was hanging outside of the church and there was big commotion. We lived right next door to the church so always played in the church parking lot on New Lots Avenue. After church a man walked up to one of the ministers in the church and cut his head off with a machete. His head came off his shoulders. Everyone started running and crying. We were in shock. I could not believe I had just seen this happen. I did not see him cut his head off but we did see the aftermath. My brothers and cousins seen the actual happen. The Church was closed for a while after this happened. When it opened back up a couple of weeks later the rumor was it was because someone was messing with someone wife. Whatever the reason was it changed the whole mood in the church. You couldn't feel the warmth anymore. We still attended the church. My new stepfather was as perverted as the last one was but even worse. He would tell me to come sit on his lap and I would feel him arise, he would tickle me and want to play fight with me. I was hoping my mom would find this behavior unacceptable but to my dismay it continued. I hated when my mom left the house because it would get worse. He would kiss me all over my neck and touch my chest and I remember hating the disgusting smoky smell on his breath from the Saratoga cigarettes he smoked. I hated him and I grew more and more any angrier every time I had to look at him knowing he was fondling me. I wonder sometime even at this adult age, why I did not seek help or reach out to my mom but I honestly didn't know how to deal with this especially as a child who was already dealing with issues from being teased all my young life first by my own siblings and cousins and then had to endure the same teasing in school with my classmates. At one point my mom moved us to the Bronx. I didn't like the Bronx at all but I was a child so what could I do. I quickly learned why I did not like the Bronx. My mom began dating a man whom I really liked. He seemed to really care about us children. He had a nice car and a beautiful apartment on Walton Avenue. He wore nice big gold chains and had rings on all his fingers. He wore suits and nice hats. I know he was into some kind of business but I didn't know what it was. He use to come to our house on Morris Avenue and bring all kinds of goodies and snacks. I remember mom would take us over his house and there was a School with a large school yard. I remember playing and running all over that school yard finally being able to be a kid. That was short lived. I remember mon taking me over his house with her and for whatever reason I was left alone with him I think my mom walked to the store I truly can't remember but I do remember he told me to come sit on his lap and he started sticking his finger in my panties. I remember thinking oh no not again. I felt like I had a sign written on my forehead saying 'COME TOUCH ME' I am writing this I had to pause for a moment almost being brought to tears at the memories. When my mom came back I was quiet but she didn't pay it any mind. I don't know what made him do this to me but I assumed since all the other men did this to me maybe it was my fault. But what could I have been doing to make this touching and fondling me keep happening I was a child. My mom use to say to me "with your fast ass" so maybe I was being to grown but what was I to do when all her grown men boyfriends are touching me. I really was suffering with some issues during that time but no one seen the depression hell I did not even know what was wrong with me I just knew I started to dislike myself. Here I am redheaded light skin with freckles I felt so ugly and different then to make matters worse I am being touched on by men and no one is seeing these signs of what's happening to me. While living in the Bronx my mom met a lady who would come over our house and have bible study. This wasn't the kind of Bible study I remembered having in Light House church. This was so different, even the book we were reading from was different. This was some religion called the "We People". They had their own set of belief and mom seemed to fall in with these people. I remember she had my mom putting salt on the floor and we had like a shrine of statues, a green fat Buda seated in a squatted position, different colors of candles, a bowl with water in it all in a corner. I never knew why mom had this stuff in the corner but I knew it had had some spiritual value to her. I personally thought it was creepy especially the green fat bald-headed man. My mom would burn incense and smoke up the whole house. We even started wearing some beads around out neck. I hated wearing these beads because we had to keep them in our shirt we weren't allow to wear them on the outside of our clothes because they were blessed and they kept evil spirits away. I remember my beads so well they were white. We had different colors but I mostly wore white ones. This lady had my mom so brainwashed that my mom kind of cut everyone off. I remember my aunt and cousins moved in with us we lived on Featherbed Lane in the Bronx. It was fun for a little while but we ended up moving back to Brooklyn. I didn't like the Bronx so I was really happy about moving back to Brooklyn. There were so many burned down building that the Bronx looked like a war zone. There was so much poverty and the sad thing about it was it was ok and acceptable by our people. They were comfortable living in the slums.

Chapter 3

Back to Brooklyn

I was so happy when we eventually moved back to Brooklyn but I was totally damaged by this time. I remember living in Flatbush and that was the beginning of the end. I became mean and wanted to fight everybody and their momma. I wasn't afraid of anyone and would fight the world. I hated my life and I wanted to die. I remember when I first got my menstruation and my mom did have the talk with me about what this meant. I wish I would have told my mom right then and there about all that I had been though. We moved to East 19th street and I had somewhat of a normal life. I met my very best friend and we are still friends to this day. I loved having a friend I could call my own friend because I felt like everything I had or anyone I cared about hurt or abused me. My best friend's mom and dad were still together. I wasn't use to this because all I had was stepfathers who found pleasure in touching me. Never loving me like a real father did their daughter. I loved her mom like my own mom. She treated me like I was her own daughter. We both had older sisters so we would act like we were sisters and our sisters were sisters. I was the baby in my family but she had a little brother. Then tragedy struck again, I remember we were getting ready to go to the pool and we were waiting for our friend to come back down stairs. She went upstairs to her house to get her bathing suit and towel. One of our friends who lived a couple of blocks over from us had a swimming pool in their back yard. We would get together and go to their house and swim. We were all waiting outside for her to come downstairs so we could go. We were ringing her bell and calling up to her window but she wouldn't answer. Some of the kids went upstairs to get her and her apartment door was open, all of a sudden one of our friends yells out the window "she's dead she's dead". Some people started running into the building but I wasn't going up there. I turned and ran down the block to tell my mom what happened. The Cops, Ambulance and fire trucks came. They blocked out street off. We were outside crying. I remember someone said they saw her boyfriend go into the building. Come to find out he stabbed her to death. The news team came out. I remember the bright lights and cameras trying to interview people. Her mom came home and it was so sad to watch her go into the building knowing she was going to see her daughter's body dead. I don't know how long it was before they brought her body out, but I know it was night time it had gotten dark outside. The block was pack with people some crying, some people we knew and a lot we didn't. Once word got out that there was a murder on East 19th street people came just to be noisy. I remember the next day when we came outside someone had sat the bloody mattress outside in front of the building for the garbage people to take. I will never forget seeing that mattress. Thinking why the super put the mattress right out in front of the building for everyone to see. I didn't get to go to her funeral. I do remember a lot of my friends went. They were very sad when they came on the block. I guessed that was why my mom would not let me go to the funeral. I had never been to a funeral before and didn't need to see my friend a little but older than me laying in a casket after having been murdered by her boyfriend. We had a dog that we loved. One thing my mom loved was having a dog. We took special care of our dogs. Having a dog as a pet was like having another sibling in the house. We treated them like family, sneaking them table food when mom wasn't looking, letting them get in our bed. We us to take Sheba on the roof to let her run and play. We did this because she didn't have to worry about running in the street and getting hit by a car. We had this happen to us when we were living in the Bronx. We had a beautiful white dog name Ikeem. Ikeem ran in the street and got hit by a car and died. We were so sad when he died so we decided the next dog we would make sure it didn't run in the street. This was a good idea or so we thought because something even worse ended up happening. My brother took her to the roof which was something we always did to walk her and let her play. My brother decided to have her chase a stick. He would throw the stick and Sheba would chase the stick and bring it back to him. This time when he threw the stick it went off the roof and before he could call her to stop her she jumped off the roof and landed on the spike fence that surrounded the back yard of our apartment building. It was the most horrific sight to see our beloved dog hanging impaled by about3 or 4 metal spikes going through her body. When she jumped she landed with such impact that the Fire department had to come and cut out the portion of fence she was impaled on. We stood out there crying for hours while they removed her and to make matters worse she was still alive when she first made contact with the fence but she eventually died while they were trying to remove the fence. I didn't think my mom cared or really loved me because I was the youngest and no attention was ever paid to me. My sister who is five years older than me was treated better than I was treated or so thought. I guess I didn't really understand the age difference between my sister and me. I felt I could do the things my sister was able to do. I became very resentful of my sister especially because I was being molested and she was in the same room with me and nothing ever happened to her. My sister was very loving and kind but I didn't see that at that time. I just saw favoritism. When we moved from East 19th street to East 21st street still in Flatbush. I kind of liked that apartment. There was a boy I liked but he was older than me. I guess I was about 12 or so by then. I was very grown and fast for my age again I know it was because I had to grow up before my time. That part of Flatbush was bad where we lived on East 21 street and Newkirk. There was a lot of drug dealing and drug users in that area. They use to hang out in my buildings hallway. The building behind my building on East 22nd street was a cut through. That's what we use to call two building that were connected back to back. You could walk from one building through the other without going outside. The back yards were connected but it was two separate buildings. The boy I liked was tall and cute. He was about 15 years old. I remember I was outside playing and this man who was the super of our building asked me to go to the store for him. I said ok and my friend and I walked to the store for him. When we came back he told me to keep the change and I think it was like 3 dollars so I split the change with my friend. I started seeing the super and my mom talk a lot when we were hanging outside and I felt he like my mom. Well I was right. My mom started hanging out in his house and he would come upstairs to our house. He was very nice but of course I was use to men being nice and next thing they feeling on my body or trying to kiss me so I stayed away from him. There was something different about him though. He treated me like a little girl because I was a little girl. He never tried to get fresh with me or never tried to make me feel uncomfortable around him. Never told me to sit on his lap or never looked at me like the others men would look at me like I was a piece of meat. I was finally happy that I could like a man that my mom liked and not have to worry about becoming their secret touching toy. The boy I liked lived in the building behind my building and I found out he was selling drugs. I didn't know too much about drugs or drug dealers but I wasn't stupid either. I think he use to sell weed. I know he use to smoke it because he use to come on my block and hang out around me and my friends and smoke his weed. I liked him he was a bad boy and he use to carry a gun on him. He showed it to use a couple of times. My friends were scared but I wasn't. I thought it was cool. My mom and the super were dating and he use to give me and my brothers money when he saw us outside. I remember my mother heard that I was hanging around the bad boy from East 22nd street and she told me she better not catch me outside talking to him. I met a few friends in his building so I would act like I was going to the store and sneak around the corner to see him. One day I was upstairs in my house about to go outside. I remember it was a summer day early afternoon. All of a sudden we heard gun shots. They sound so close like they were in the building… and they were. We lived on the second floor and everybody in the house went running into the hallway to see what happened. When I got downstairs there was a young boy laying against the wall in the hallway. He had been shot. I had never seen anyone shot before. They were putting towels on him and telling him to breath. My mother told us to go back upstairs in the house. The ambulance and cops came and took him away. The super was cleaning up the blood in the hallway when I went back downstairs. All my friends were outside waiting for me to come out. They didn't live in my building so they were standing outside but the people who lived in the building the cops wouldn't let us in or out of the building. When I got outside everybody was talking about the shooting and I found out the boy I liked shot the boy in my hallway. They had a beef in his building and he chased him through the building backyard into my building. I never saw the boy I liked again. The super of my building and my mom became a couple and my siblings and I loved him. He treated my mom so good and he treated us good to. To this very day we still love him. My mom and grandpa were together for over 35 years. All the grandkids and great grandkids call him grandpa. Even after moms death in June/2015 we still have grandpa in our lives. He have been the closest man to having a father in my life.

Chapter 4

Too Much Pain for a Child

My public school years weren't that great so I figured now I am headed to junior high school it would be a lot better. I was happy because in junior high school we got a chance to walk the halls and which classes when the bell rang. I also liked being able to see my friends who were in other classes. We would stop and talk in the hall for a few minutes before the second bell rang which was the late bell. I was excited about going to junior high school. I went to Walt Whitman junior high school in Flatbush. I was already miss popular. By this time I knew a lot of people in Flatbush. Even though I was young I had 2 brothers and a cousin who knew everyone in the neighborhood. My brothers and my cousin whom my mom raised after his mom died in 1979 he became a brother to me. He was older then my brothers so we looked up to him like he was the older brother. I was also very popular because of the color of my hair which I still didn't like but I was a little better with the way I look. I still hated having different color hair then the rest of the world. I felt so ugly. I was light skinned with orange hair and freckles on my face and hands. I use to wish I had black hair and dark skin. I was the only person in my entire generation who had red hair. I was told my dad side of the family had red hair but I never met any of them so how did I know that was true. I thought if I had met them I would have felt better knowing I wasn't the only person in the world who looked like this but I didn't know anything about my father but what I last remember when I was a little girl. I wished I had my own father when I was growing up because I don't think those men would have did the things they did to me. I think he would have protected me from my molesters. By Junior High School I was totally depressed. I didn't even know this because I truly didn't know what depression was. I just knew I was making wrong choices in my life and I wasn't even grown yet. Though I use to smile a lot an act like I was happy, deep down inside I was really unhappy inside. I really didn't know how to deal with my feeling because I didn't know what I was feeling. I just know I would be happy on the outside but inside I felt sad. When I was in school it took me out of my element so I was able to function as a normal child. But when I had my alone time or down time I would start remembering being touched and the fear that I felt when it would happen to me. I would then experience another bout of depression wondering why no one saw the signs, why no one helped me, why no one cared about me. Then the anger would set in and I would shut down or lash out. Normally lasing out was easier for me because I would release my hurt and pain that was inside of me on someone else and I would get attention. Even if it meant getting in trouble for my lashing out at least for a moment I felt like somebody cared about me. Even if just for a moment. I also started getting attention from boys a lot. I didn't know why because there were so many pretty girls around but I notice the boys started liking me. And boy "O "boy was I glad about that. Looking back I guess I was glad when boys really started to like me because before that all my attention came from men that where older than me but now here I am getting attention from boys my own age or a little older. I already knew how to kiss and I was good at it or so my so called first boyfriend who shot someone told me. I started becoming more aware of my sexuality because of the molestation so now I knew how to explore my own body. I had feelings that I knew weren't normal for a child my age to have. I began to realize why I liked Junior High School so much. I started liking the school janitor. All the girls liked him. He was very handsome had the cutest bow legs, nice soft curly hair and the most beautiful almond complexion. I use to see him watching me as I walked the halls changing classes or just hanging out in the hall way. I didn't think he liked me because there were so many pretty more advanced girls then me. Every time we saw each other we would smile always making eye contact. One time he winked at me. My friend said that meant he liked me. One day I saw him in the hallway when I was going to the bathroom. The hall way was relatively empty most of the students were in class. When he saw me coming down the hallway he started smiling. As I got closer to him he said you are very pretty. No one had ever told me I was pretty actually it was quite the opposite. I was so use to being teased about my looks that I couldn't believe he thought I was pretty. I was so use to older men taking advantage of me but this seemed different. He seemed different from the dirty old men I was used to. I thought he was talking to someone behind me so I turned and look to see who was coming. I actually told him I liked him and you would think him being a grown man would have turned down my advances but nope he told me he liked me as well. Now I had a reason to love school. I looked forward to seeing him in school. One thing led to another and I found myself kissing and humping him in the Janitors closet on a regular bases. We never had sex but I enjoyed him kissing and feeling on my developing breast. I thought he was really feeling me until I found out he was messing with another young classmate. She was telling everyone in class that she was dating him. To top it all off he was married. I decided I wanted to fight her my classmate because I felt she was disrespecting me by messing with my man actually she was seeing him before I was. So technically I was messing with her man who again is married. I gathered a couple of my friends and we went to her house to fight her in East Flatbush. I knew where she lived because we were friends and I had been to her house before. The reason I decided to go to her house to fight her was because I didn't want to get into trouble or get him into trouble. I had put the word out that I wanted to fight her so I didn't see her in school forma couple of days. Now I was a bully and liked to start trouble with kids in school. Why because I felt angry with all the stuff I been through in my young life so I just had this I don't care attitude. I liked fighting since I did so much of it as a child. I remember when we were living with the pervert on Hendrix Street. I was in Public School 213 and I was teased constantly because of my red hair. I would come home crying just about every day from being teased and I remember my mom told me if anyone tease you punch them in their face. Now we came from a fighting family so this wasn't uncommon for this to be my mom reaction. Growing up spending my early years in the projects you had to fight. So now my mom gave me permission to fight anyone that teased me and I did. When I was teased I would hit first and didn't care if I got in trouble because my mom said it was ok. I had plenty of fights in P.S and I was still very young. So now here I am in Junior High School and my mom created a monster. I loved to fight and always hit first. So back to my janitor boyfriend, I called myself not wanting to fight on the school premises. So if the school found out we were fighting over him he could get in a lot of trouble. When we got to her house one of my friends rang her bell to get her to come outside. She lived in a two family house and was able to look out the window and see us outside in front of her house. She was afraid to come out and fight me which put a battery in my back because I knew she was scared of me. She came toschool days later and told me she was leaving him alone. She must have told him what I did to her because he was upset with me. When I saw him he didn't speak to me. When I was finally able to ask him why he was upset with me and he said because of me putting our business in the school. I remember about a month later I didn't see him anymore in school. I had his beeper number but he wasn't answering when I beeped him. I later found out my friend who was messing with him her mom made a complaint and there were other young girls in the school he was messing around with and here it is I thought I was special. He ended up getting transferred from the school. I was devastated because he was my first so called love. My friend and I made up and we became good friends throughout our Junior High School years.

Chapter 5

I Just Don't Care Anymore

By now I had developed a bad attitude not caring about nothing so I began to exhibit this destructive behavior in my first of three Junior High Schools. I remember when the West Indians began to come into America and we use to tease them because the way they dressed and wore their hair. I was miss popularity in school so had a lot of followers. People wanted to be my friend just because I didn't take no crap. I use to fight other peoples battles. When there was a fight going down and if my friends was involved I would jump in the fight and help them beat up the person they were fighting. There was a new girl in my class and I didn't like her for no reason. She was quiet and didn't talk much so I started picking on her. Once I started picking on her the rest of the class use to brother her. We use to call her names and tease her about her glasses. She started hanging out with some girls who didn't like me. They wouldn't mess with me because they knew I had a crew of friends but they didn't like me because I was a bully. They pushed the scary chick up to fight me knowing they were too scared to step to me. They started going around the school saying they wanted to fight me and they were going to jump me one day when they could catch me by myself. I was very rarely alone except when I walked to school in the mornings sometimes. But most of the time I was with my crew. I decided to carry a knife just in case they ever tried to fight me and I was alone I would be able to defend myself. I wasn't scared of them but I wasn't going to be caught slipping up either. Ok so what possessed me to take my mom butcher knife and put it in my book bag and carry it around with me every day in school. I clearly wasn't thinking the hurt or damage I could cause someone if I stabbed them with the knife. I don't think I really cared either. Walt Whitman I had a fight with a young lady who wanted to fight me just because I was popular and had a lot of friends. I remember coming out the school and there was a crowd very usual for after school recess. People started coming up to me telling me the girl wanted to fight me. I didn't even know why she wanted to fight me because we stopped teasing her but I knew her and her friends didn't like me and my friends. I always use to tease the new comers or freshmen that came into the school because I felt that was my school and I knew everybody but I didn't really take it out on one person, everyone was subject to being teased for being a new jack. I do remember teasing her about her sneakers and no name brand clothes but again I didn't think nothing of it. Well she must have thought much about it because she put the word out that she wanted to fight me. Well this particular day I had to stay after school in the discipline room for one of my disruption behavior outburst I was very well known for. When I came out the school all my peeps were telling me she was waiting after school for me but because I had to stay late she left and said she was going to fight me tomorrow. My friends waited to tell what was going on so I could be prepared for her the next day. So I said ok tomorrow I am going to confront her. The next day I put the word out that I was going to beat her up after school. After school I gathered a group of my friends together just in case her friends tried to jump in while I was beating her up I wanted to make sure my back was covered. We saw her walking out of the school. She was by herself which was a surprise to me. I felt her friends heard I was going to beat her up so they got scared and didn't want no parts of me and my crew. We followed her down the block from the school. I went up to her and said I heard you want to fight me. She ignored me. I should have walked away then but my friends were instigating and telling me to hit her. I walked up behind her and said it again I thought you want to fight me and she ignored me again. This time I took both my hands and pushed her as hard as I could in her back but again she kept walking. I use to wear a name buckle belt, those belts were very popular back then. The belt would have your name encased in a gold plated buckle. Mines said 'RED' which was my nickname everyone called me. I took the belt off and wrapped the strap of the belt around my hand and let the buckle hang. As I followed her down the street trying to pick a fight with her she just continued to walk and ignore me. Now, I had taken one of my mother's steak knives out of the kitchen and I snuck it into my book bag that morning. Since I heard the day before they planned on fighting me. I really don't know to this day why I made that decision to put that knife in my bag. I was carrying it before but I took it out of my bag. But that morning I put it back in my bag. Also, I was at a I don't care place in my young life. I was known for carrying a weapon but I had never used one on anyone before. I guess I wanted to scare her not really intending to use the knife. I was use to men taking advantage of me so it was a sort of defense mechanism if anyone tried to hurt or violate me again. As I pushed her in the back again this time she turned around as though she was going to swing at me. I swung the belt buckle as hard as I could and hit her across her face with the buckle of the belt. I will never forget hearing the cracking sound of the belt coming into contact with her face. I swung the belt so hard that the buckle flew off the belt. I thought that was the end of the fight but she came charging at me like a wild bull. I started running backwards to get away from her because she had blood on her face. I ran around a car not knowing what to do but she was on my heels. The next thing I know someone handed me my book bag which had the knife in it. I remember telling people I had the knife even showing the knife off at school that day that's how the person knew to pass me my bag. I grabbed the knife out of my bag and turned around and said something like what you going to do now. Well to my surprise she came charging at me even though I had the knife in my hand. The next thing I remember is throwing the knife at her not in no way thinking it would make contact with her being that I threw it and not physically stabbed her with it. Well I looked and she grabbed her side and fell forward screaming and crying I remember seeing blood on her shirt and I thought what had I done. My best friend picked up our book bags and I still had the knife in my hand and we started running. My victim she is now running towards the school. I see the school guards come running out the school I guess someone had told them what happened. My friend and I ran really with no direction. I knew I was in trouble. I was scared to go home and she being a true friend ran away with me. I had several best friends growing up. I was always able to make and keep friends. This best friend was an only child and she and I because inseparable. We would spend the night at each other house. We wore each other clothe. We were like sisters well we considered each other to be sisters that's how close we were. We were so close that we cut our fingers and rubbed the blood together and became blood sisters when we first met in this same Junior High School. We are still best friends to this very day. So now we done ran away from the school and we didn't have any place to go. We didn't know what to do so we roamed the streets until it got dark. Once it got dark we went to Kings County Hospital to hang out in the lobby where we knew no one would bother us. As night fell when we got tired we took turns sleeping so one of us would be woke to protect and watch each other. She had no reason to run away with me. I was the one who was in trouble but she stuck by my side as a real friend did. Honestly I don't know if I would have done the same thing for her. But I did appreciate having the company with me. Having someone to go through this ordeal with me was so endearing because all the other trauma I went through in my life I went through it alone.

Chapter 6

More Self-Destruction

Boy, that bench was so hard and uncomfortable. I wanted to go home so bad and get in my bed but I was scared. I didn't know if she lived or was very seriously hurt all I knew was I was in trouble. I still had the knife in my book bag that goes to show you that I didn't anything about being a criminal because I still had the evidence in my book bag. We sat up talking for a while. I tried to sleep but I was so worried about what happened to the girl I cut cut/stabbed. Now the question became what are we going to do and where are we going to go once day light arrived. We had a friend who we knew stayed home and took care of her little brother who was disabled. She was a few years older than we were. I met her through my cousin who was going with her at the time. She was his girlfriend. We use to go to her house and cut school and hang out so we knew her mom was working during the school hours. Once we got to her house we told her all about what happened at school with the stabbing the day before. She told us that our mothers were was calling all my friends mothers looking for us and that our families were worried about us. She made us some breakfast and allowed us to go to sleep being that we really didn't sleep all night. While we were sleeping she called my mom told her we were at her house. We awoke to my two uncles standing over us telling us to get up they were taking us straight to the precinct the girl pressed charges on me and the cops were looking for me. I was shocked scared nervous ashamed and almost became sick to my stomach. I had never been to a precinct before so I truly didn't know what to expect. When we got to the 69th precinct which was the precinct close to my school and served that district, my best friends mom and dad where there waiting for her. The officer took us into a room and hand-cuffed us to a steel pole mounted to the wall. Because we were minors they allowed her parents to come into the room they had us in. Her mom walked up to her and slapped her face so hard I felt it across the room where I was cuffed to the pole as well. I felt real bad for her because she was in trouble because of me. They ended up releasing her from the precinct before releasing me, because she really didn't do anything she just ran away from home with me. They kept me for hours I guess to scare me into thinking I was going to jail which I was really petrified. After a couple of hours they released me into my two uncles who were still waiting for me in the waiting area. When I got home I just knew my mon was going to beat the skin off of me but to my surprise she just put me on punishment for the entire summer. I guess she wanted to wait and see what happened to me when went to court. I will never forget the fear I felt about going to court. I wasn't allowed back into school until the court hearing came. I was expelled pending the outcome of the court hearing. During the time I was out of school which was only a matter of weeks. My mom went up to the school and they gave me a homework package they prepared for me to do at home. I missed being in school, I missed my friends, plus as tough as I tried to act I was concerned about my classmate. I already knew she had to be admitted in the hospital but I didn't know the damage I caused. I found out that she lived a few blocks from me on Ditmas Avenue. I didn't know where she lived when we were in school. I was shocked to find out she lived so close. I wish I could have went to her house to tell her I was sorry but I knew I had to stay away from her. I really didn't know much about what was going on about the court case because they were dealing with my mom. My court date finally came and I was so scared. we went to Family Court Downtown Brooklyn. I tried to act brave in front of my family but I was scared. I had only seen the inside of a court room on television and even then it looked scary. The big judge sitting up there in a robe and banging that piece of stick on the desk. I felt the Court room the Judge the whole process was so scary. When we got to court I remember the room looked huge. The judge seat was high above the rest of the courtroom. There were court officers in the court room I guessed just in case people acted up. I saw her sitting across the room with who I assumed was her family. I tried to make eye contact with her but she wouldn't look at me. When the judge came into the courtroom the whole court had to stand up. I thought to myself why do we have to stand up for him to come into the room. He is not the president of the United Stated of America. As we were sitting there a man who I found out was my legal aid lawyer came to talk to us. He took us into a small room to talk and ask what exactly happened. I told him the trust that I hit her first and that I hit her with the belt buckle. He was looking at me like are you crazy, you sitting here admitting your total and absolute guilt in this case. I didn't know, he asked me what happened and I told him. He told me and my mom that I could get sent away for six months to Spofford Juvenile Detention. Spofford was the jail for young people I think under 16. I had heard a lot about Spofford. It was a bad place for bad kids. I sure didn't want to go to Spofford this was my first time in any kind of serious trouble. He said something about the judge could ask me questions. I don't think I understood the full extent of what was happening because I remember saying well I am just going to tell him what happened. Well he explained because I took the knife to school meant I had intentions on using it and I followed her and hit her first. I was crying by this time because I didn't realize how serious this was. He said to me if the judge finds out that meant to stab her I would get sent away. My best friend came there with her mom and dad and we all sat together. I didn't even know she had to come to court because I wasn't able to talk to her since the incident happened. I found out her mother sent her to live with her grandmother. I didn't know she was named the case as well. She didn't deserve to be in this trouble. She didn't do anything but supported me, but because she was with me she was involved in the case. I was happy to see her just to see a familiar face and to know again she was at my side. When the judge called my case the lawyers went up to talk first. Then they called me up and I wanted to pee on myself. The judge told me to sit down next to him in the seat on this side of Judge seat. The judge asked me my name and age and I told him. I remember the court officer came over to me and I had to put my hand on the Bible and swear to tell the truth the whole truth and nothing but the truth so help me God. I looked at the girl from off the stand and she was looking at me this time. I felt really bad for her. I remember wanting to tell her I was sorry but we could not have any contact with each other. I did not know that she ended up spending several days in the hospital and she had stitches in her stomach where the knife stuck her. My bravado was gone and I felt like an ant. I did not realize the extent of pain I caused someone but then again I wasn't thinking that way. As a child I had been subjected to so much pain myself. I remember the judge asking me to tell my side of the story. I thought about what the lawyer told me about getting sent to Spofford. I thought about being locked away for six months. I thought about why did I take the knife to school, why did I pull it out of my bag, why did I use it, why? SO I lied through my teeth. I told the Judge she hit me first and I had to defend myself. I was afraid of her. She was going around the school saying they was going to jump me so I brought the knife to protect myself. I started crying and they were real tears. I was crying for my freedom and I was truly scared of him sending me to juvenile jail. I didn't realize the extent of telling a lie especially after putting my hand on the Holy Bible. After I was done they called my best friend up and she lied as well. She said the girl hit me first also. I couldn't believe she was really up there lying foe me. Then they called some other classmates who witnessed the incident. I did not know they had done an investigation and went to the school to talk to kids who witnessed the fight. They had to come to court to testify about what they saw. Everybody lied for me I couldn't believe it. Even though I felt bad for her I was happy people came to court and lied for me. The judge extended the order of protection for her. I couldn't go near her. I couldn't go back to the school they had expelled me from the school and the judge ordered me to go to the school out of my zone school, and they put me on probation for 6 months. I didn't care as long as I didn't have to go to Spofford. As I was coming off the judge bench I looked at her but she had her head down. I really felt even worse because she didn't deserve what I did to her and to make it worse we made it seem like she started it. I still don't understand how I got out of that situation. This is when I think God started covering me with his favor because each person got up there and said she hit Vanessa first. I could not believe it. The Judge told me in front of the entire court that I was lucky because I took the knife with intent to use it but because I was defending myself he would put me out of the school and give her an order of protection against me. Then then went on to tell me that he could have given me six months in Spofford Juvenile Facility which at that time was the worst facility in New York to house troubled youths. Only God could have brought me through.

Chapter 7

Remorse

Let me just say I took no pleasure in remembering the details of this part of my past. I caused harm to someone who truly didn't deserve it. I could have really hurt her and she could have died. I could have thrown my whole life away in the blink of an eye. I am truly sorry for this part of my past. There was a Television show that use to come on some years ago. The show was called 'Forgive or Forget". The show aired from (1985-2000). The host of the show was a lady who went by the name 'Mother Love". The show was designed for people who felt other people wronged them or they were wronged by other people and they want to apologize to the person they did wrong to or demand an apology from someone else. The show was a real tear jerker. I cried several times watching the show as well as Mother love and the audience. There is nothing like seeing people make up after carrying hurt and pain around. The catcher of the show was if the person were going to accept the other person apology they would appear at the door when it opened but if they weren't ready to accept the apology they would not appear. Most of the time it always ended in a success with the people making up. I loved the show a lot of family and broken relationships were repaired. Mother Love was a kind and gentle lady who would put you in the mind of your grandmother. She reminded me of a grandmother who would hug you and bury your face in her bosom and while stroking your hair while telling you everything is going to be alright. I was sad when the show went off the air because it was a good show.

When I first saw the show I said I wanted to go on the show and apologize to people I have hurt and ask for their forgiveness. I always said I would love to go on that show before the entire world I would apologize to my school mate for stabbing her. I am still sorry for my actions to this very day sorry. I chose not to use her name because I want to respect her privacy but again I am truly sorry for all the hurt and pain I cause her and her family. I know if there is still a scar on her stomach every time she sees that scar she remembers how she got it. Again I am truly sorry. Sorry does not express how even to this day over 30 years later how remorseful I still am. I f I ever see her again I would drop to my knees and whole heartedly beg her forgiveness. Even if she choose not to accept my apology I will feel better about being woman enough to tell her I am sorry. It crazy because as big as the world is yet it is still small and I have never ran into her. I use to wonder when I was a teenager and into my young adulthood how I would handle it if I was to run into her. When I was younger I felt if she was to run up on me I would be ready to fight her. As I got older I began to grow up especially after I became a mother. I began to mature and realize that I had to leave the streets alone. I had to change my stinking thinking and grow up. I realized my actions could have affected the rest of her life. She could have grown up bitter or with a lot of resentment. She could have developed a fear of knives or being assaulted. Actually I haven't seen her since junior high school so I don't know how her life turned out. I hope and pray that all is well and all the best for her. Hopefully she became a mother and a grandmother like God has blessed me with. The reality is we don't think about these things until we get older and sit back and do an inventory of our lives. Then we end up having a case of the shoulda, coulda, wouda which is what I ended up having. So many regrets, so many tears, so much heartache and still so much more regrets, more tears and more heartache to come. If someone had told me I would go through as much as I am about to tell you about, I would have told them they are lying to me. Of course I was not allowed to go back to Walt Whitman J.H.S. which I was upset about. All my friends were there and I didn't want to go to a new school. I would have to make new friends. I wished at that very moment that this would have never happened but it was too late. I was happy I didn't have to go to a juvenile detention center. If I had to choose I would have picked a new school over jail any day. I was truly blessed because it could have been so much worse for me. I wasn't a hard core criminal. I was just a little girl who had so many bad breaks in her young life that she was looking for attention in all the wrong places. After being kicked out of Walt Whitman J.H.S. I was transferred to Ditmas J.H.S. I was kind of happy when I got to Ditmas because come to find out I knew a lot of kids there. But that was kind of a problem as well because I wasn't compelled to learn. I quickly feel in with the rowdy crowd. To make matters worse everyone knew about my incident in Whitman so now I was some sort of a celebrity but all for the wrong reasons. Ditmas and Walt Whitman were the two Junior High Schools that served the Flatbush area so everybody from the community went to either or. I was living on East 21st street at this time. I really didn't want to be in Ditmas even though I knew everyone I didn't like change so I decided I wasn't going to do anything in school but show up. During the summer months my mom would send me to the Bronx to spend the summer with very close family friends. I guess my mom thought it was better to get me out of the neighborhood for the summer to keep me out of trouble. I started messing with this older guy on my block East 21street. My friend was messing with his brother. We thought we were grown because the older drug dealers liked us. I was very new to the drug dealing business. They weren't into what is considered hard drugs. They only sold marijuana as far as I knew. His dad was the super of the building they lived in. He would sneak the key from his father and take me in the basement. In the basement was a room with a bed in it. He would lock the elevator so it wouldn't come down to the basement. The basement was where the garbage was kept so the tenants would come down there to empty the garbage. We would go down there and kiss. After that got boring he tried to get me to go further with him but I wasn't ready. I liked when he kissed and sucked my breast but I wasn't ready to have sex with him. I liked him a lot but I knew he had a girlfriend. I knew he just wanted to get in my panties. He ran his mouth about me being in the basement with him and my brothers found about it. My oldest brother confronted him and told him he better leave me alone because he was too old for me. I guess he was scared of my brother because he would see me and walk right pass me. I was pissed off because I felt my brother needed to mind his business. Also how he was in the basement with me and now you going to walk right pass me like you don't even know me. Then his girlfriend use to walk pass me and roll her eyes so I guess she heard about him and I. I was glad I did not sleep with him because she was pregnant but he never told me that. My friend and his brother really liked each other and they started officially going together. His brother was younger than him so him. Actually my friend was older than his brother. They stayed together for years and now have a son together. Over the years my friend ended up moving to Durham North Carolina. We lost contact for many years. One day I ended up running into her on a visit to New York. She told me she was thinking about moving back here. I asked her what ever happened to Mr. S is we'll call him.She told me that they broke up her and his brother and last she heard my old boyfriend was in jail. I told her to get this address so I could write him in jail. We lost contact again you know how that go use say we will keep in touch but end up not staying in contact. Again some time went by and my mom moved off of St. Johns and it just so happens that she lived on the same block my mom moved on which is where my mom still live well until she died 2015 but my sister still have the apartment. I jumped ahead of myself but I had to in order to tell this part of my life. So she gives me his jail information and I write him. He writes me back and now we are corresponding with each other through letters. He asked me to come see him and I told him I would.

Chapter 8

Looking for Love

I went to see him in Arthur Kill Correctional Facility in Staten Island. I was scared and excited at the same time. I hadn't seen him in over twenty years. I remembered how cute he was when we were younger but I didn't know what he looked like now. I remember when I went to see him. I hadn't been to a jail to visit anyone so I didn't know what it entailed. I had to take off my shoes, walk through a metal detector and get scanned by an officer. That wasn't even the worse part. The worse part was the dog they brought on the bud to sniff around the bus. I was appalled that I had to sit there while a dog sniffed around looking for drugs. Right then and there I knew this wouldn't be an often thing for me. I felt I was too cute to go through this humiliation. Especially for someone I hadn't seen in years. Once inside the jail we had to put all of our belonging in a locker. We were then put into a big waiting room. I remembered what he looked like but as I said I hadn't seen him in many years. Once I noticed him I was like DAMN!! HE'S STILL FINE AS HE WAS BACK IN THE DAY. He was always bowlegged but it looked even sexier watching him walk towards me. I got up and gave him a hug. I was really happy to see him. He was definitely happy to see me. I made sure I was dressed to impress. We reminisced about old times in the basement of his building. I told him all about what I had been through since last seeing him. He told me about his drug charge. I must say I had a really good time on the visit. I paid for us to take pictures, we got food out of the vending machine and we went outside into a yard that the prisoners are allowed to take the visitors. When the visit was over he asked me if I would come back to see him again. I told him I would love to. I always liked him but I was just too young for him plus he had a girlfriend. It would be easy to fall for him again now that I was older. I could see myself rekindling the feeling the old feeling I had for him. I left the visit feeling good. Especially because It was good seeing an old friend. We started writing each other on a regular basis. I went up there that following weekend to see him and again we had a great time. We played cards and took pictures. I looked forward to by visits with him and it really wasn't far away. I would take the Staten Island Ferry and take a bus when I got to Staten Island. A couple of months went by and I was going to see him like every two weeks. Things were going good between us so I thought, we weren't an official couple after all he was in jail but I felt we were trying to build something so when he got out of jail we could see what was up with us being a couple. It wasn't like we were strangers we knew each other for many years. One day I decided to surprise him and go see him without telling him I was coming. I would normally go every two weeks but I felt like going to see him on the off weekend that I normally wouldn't go. I was happy because I assumed he would be happy and surprised to see me. My hair was freshly done, nails done, clothes crisp, looking good ready for my visit. When I went up to the desk to register I was told he already had a visit. I'm like already have a visitor. I had become cool with a few of the Correction Officers from going up there so often. One of the officers who I was cool with was on duty that day. She told me he was on a visit with a girl. I was like are you serious. She looked on the log and told me that girl comes up there all the time on the weeks that I don't come. I couldn't believe that he had me and her coming on alternate weeks. He didn't think I would ever find out because I didn't normally come on this weekend. I was livid. Because he was lying to me. I didn't care if he had someone because we had just gotten back in contact after many years so I really didn't expect him to be single. He was to fine not to have someone in his life. My issue with him was him not being honest with me. I couldn't wait to write him and tell him off. I wrote him and told him I came up there and couldn't get to see him because he had a visitor and how pissed off I was because I wasted my time and money coming all the way up there just to have to turn around and come back home. On top of that I thought he was single which we had discussed on a visit. He wrote me back and told me she was his ex-girlfriend and they were not together anymore and she came up there to put money in his commissary and bring him weed. I decided this wasn't worth it plus I was not about to get myself into any trouble trying to sneak some drugs into a jail and end up locked up my darn self. He wasn't going to stop seeing her if she was suppling him with money and drugs so let her be stupid because I wasn't doing it. He had the nerve to write and ask me if I would do what she was doing then he would stop her from coming to visit him. I didn't answer his letter and after a while he stopped writing me and I stopped writing him. Just as fast as that chapter of my life was reopened it was closed. My mom felt she needed to send me away for the summer. I guess she thought getting me out of the neighborhood would be good for me. She had a very close friend who lived in the Bronx. My family and the White family were like blood relatives. We would have family picnics, Birthday parties, and BBQs together. I don't know how long my mom knew their family but I do know as long as I could remember our families were always friends. At first I didn't want to go to the Bronx because I loved my neighborhood and my friends. Once I started going I loved it up there. I started spending weekends up there and before I knew it I was asking my mom could I go up there. I also liked going to the Bronx because I had a chance to get out of the house considering I was always on punishment. In the Bronx I had more freedom. We were able to hang out in front of the building until it got late. I loved their block Sedgwick Avenue. In all that I had been through I didn't know my world was about to take another turn for the unknown. When were outside hanging out I would notice the older boys were hanging out in front of the building next to my friends building. They were different from the guys I was use to seeing. They wore a lot of jewelry and dressed in nice clothes. Their Hats, Shirts, Pants and Sneakers all matched. They were fly. There was one who every time I walked passed him, he would say something to me like "pretty girl" or I like you. I would always smile and keep walking because it was always a lot of them and I wasn't really shy but I was nervous. Not a nervous scared but a nervous like wow he like me. My friend knew some of them and she told me they owned the weed spot in the building. They looked like they didn't have regular jobs. They were flashy. Drinking beer and playing a loud Boom box radio that you could hear all the way at the corner of the block. One day we were outside and we decided to walk to the store. I wanted to go to the store just so I could walk pass the older boys. I had already decided I was going to talk to him if he tried to talk to me that day. I was going home in a few weeks and I kind of wanted to get to know why he liked me before I left and came back to Brooklyn. I knew he was older than me but I didn't know how much older he was. I think that's why felt I like I wanted to get to know him because I was use to older men taking advantage of me from my childhood. This time when he tried to talk to me I smiled at hi. When we were coming back from the store as I passed him he said "what's your name". I told him my name and stood there for a little while talking to him. He told me his name was Fino. I was thinking to myself who names their child fino. What an ugly name. Well fino was his street name his real name was Johnny. He asked me how old I was and I lied and told him I was 16 but I was 14yrsold about to be 15 in July. I asked him how old was he and he said much older then you. I said well I still want to know and he said 22yrs old. He asked me if I think he was too old for me and again miss fast tail said no. So he asked me if I had a beeper and I told him no. Everyone had beepers back then but I of course didn't have one. I was too young to have a beeper plus my momma wasn't about to buy my grown tail a beeper. I didn't even know how a beeper worked but he was soon about to show me. He gave me his beeper number and told me how to use it. I just had to make sure I used a phone that he could call me back on. Later that night I beeped him from their house phone and he called me right back. He knew it was me because he gave me a code number to use. He asked me could I come outside and I told him after they went to sleep I would try to sneak out. My family friends had a three bedroom apartment. There were two daughters and two sons. I was sleeping in the room with the daughters. Me and the younger daughter use to go hang. We were closer in age. We started sneaking out of the house after her mom went to sleep to hang out with the older guys from the building next door. One night we snuck out and was hanging out with them in the courtyard of their building and they invited us into their apartment. Come to find out their apartment was where they sold weed from. I knew all about marijuana but I never tired smoking it before. My friend did tell me that they sold drugs but I had never been inside of an actual drug spot. I would see them outside smoking weed right in front of the building like it was legal. My fast tail was way too eager to go hang in the illegal weed spot. It was a regular apartment but it had iron gates on the backyard windows. It wasn't really furnished like an apartment would be. I remember two mixed matched couches and a carpet on the floor. A table and a TV, but there were no pictures on the walls it didn't have a home feeling like

I was us to. My friend fino and his friend lived in the weed spot. I saw a cat walking around and I hated cats. We never had a cat growing up we always had dogs. I asked him to out the cat up because I didn't like cats and he did. He offered us something to drink. They were drinking Old English 800 beer and I took a glass and so did my friend. I liked it though it was strong I liked drinking it. It made me feel like I was grown. We didn't stay out long because we didn't want her mom to wake up and see we were not in the house but we told them we would come hang out with them tomorrow. We started hanging out in the weed spot on a regular going there in the early afternoon while her mom was at work. His friend liked my friend so it was cool the four of us chilling together. They would roll up their weed and smoke but we weren't smoking weed at the time, but of course once we started hanging in the spot we decided to try smoking weed with them. I remember my first time smoking I coughed so hard I thought I was going to pass out, but I loved it. It made me feel mellow like I was floating on air.

Chapter 9

An Introduction to the Drug Game

I started looking forward to going to the weed spot to hang out with the older guys. I was catching feelings for my friend. I liked him a lot just from hanging around him the past couple of weeks. He always asked me if I was hungry or if I had money. Of course I said yes I was hungry and no I didn't have any money. He would give me $5 or $10 dollars for my pocket. Now keep in mind we are talking about in the very early eighties like 1981 1982 when having $5 or $10 dollars in your pocket was a lot of money. I knew I would be going back to Brooklyn soon summer was almost over and school would be back before you knew it. I knew I was going to miss my new friend and I was sad to have to go home. We were feeling ourselves being young and catching the eye of older drug dealers. Plus they loved having us young girls around. I guess it fed their ego. Either way it was a winning situation for us all. Johnny (fino) ended up becoming my first born son's father but well get to that part of my life later. Fino introduced me to adulthood way to early. I wasn't no sprung chicken to the streets but I wasn't really out there like that. He was eight years older than I was and far more advanced. He knew the ends and outs of the street life and I like that. Every day we would go hang out in the weed spot. All the older females who like the older guys, were mad at us for coming around their boyfriends. After all we were young and fresh meat for the older guys. I wasn't afraid of any of them and was always ready to fight if anyone said anything to me, Plus Fino had my back because I was his little hot redhead. He once told me he loved Bruce Lee, his cat named ginger and me. I thought that was so cute. My friend and I would get all the free weed we wanted from him. Sneaking out every night because a ritual since we had to go in the house at a certain time, but once Mrs. White went to sleep we would sneak back out the house. One time she was sleeping on the couch in the living room which you had to pass the living room to get to the front door. I think she was hip to use sneaking so we decided to climb down the fire scape I swear it was so much fun. Mind you they lived on the fifth floor. The guys helped us jump from the ladder onto the pavement. We only did that once though it was scary and fun at the same time. My friends mother use to drink a lot and when she got drunk she would do two things. First, she would curse us out. Then she would fall out and sleep like a drunken sailor. We would wait like thirty minutes then we would creep out the house. Back in day there was always a schoolyard jam to go to. We would find ourselves at all of the block parties. Those were the days when you could stay out until wee hours in the morning and not worry about the jam getting shot up. The DJ's would plug the speakers into the lamp pole and we would party for hours. They use to have the battles of the DJ's. They would set up two sound systems set up across from each other in the school yard and battle each other. The purpose of the battle was to get the crowd to come to your side of the yard. The fun part was running back and forth across the school yard to whoever was playing the best song at the time. When the summer was over I hated having to come back to Brooklyn. I end up falling in love with being in the the Bronx, or the freedom I had in the Bronx. When I left to come back to Brooklyn fino brought me a beeper so he could stay in touch with me. I knew I had to hide it from my mom because she would have wanted to know who gave me a beeper and why. Once back to my boring life, school started back and I wasn't happy. I wanted to be with my new boyfriend who was eight years older than me. He was officially my boyfriend as far as I was concerned. I had spent the last month of my summer vacation with him and I really was feeling him. When I got home I was happy to see my family. My friends were happy I was back from the Bronx. I had to fill them in on all I had done over the summer and show off my New beeper of course. Now, here I am in a school I don't really want to be in and in love with a guy I can't see so now I really depressed. One day while in school I was talking during class as I usually did. Disturbing and distracting the kids that did want to learn because I wasn't interested in being in school or learning. I was running my mouth and my teacher told me to be quiet. I gave him that who you talking to look. Well I continued to run my chops and he again told me to stop talking. I continued to talk so he moved my seat by the window. I felt like he was trying to embarrass me in front of the class. As I continued to mouth off he said keep talking and I'm going to throw this eraser at your mouth. I dared him to throw the eraser at me and kept talking especially now because I was pissed off that he played me in front of the class. Well before I knew it he threw the eraser across the room and it barely touched my pink Izod Lacoste shirt I had on and all hell broke loose. I picked up the chair I was sitting in and charged him with the chair swinging the chair as I was charging at him. One of my classmates tried to grab the chair from me but the leg of the chair hit my teacher in the ear. His ear began to bleed and I grabbed my book bag to run out the school but by the time I got to the door School Safety literally picked me up off my feet and carried me to the main office. I'm cursing and screaming all kinds of profanity. The principle took me into his office. I was crying and screaming that the teacher hit me with the eraser. Luckily I did have a little dust from the eraser on my shirt. Now I really didn't have any intentions on hitting my teacher with the chair but I am truly glad my classmate intervened because I was truly out of control. I knew I could not get into any more trouble after the warning the judge gave me so I just kept crying saying he hit me first. I remember they called my mom and said she had to come get me because they were going to call the police. The ambulance came and were treating him which was just a small cut on his ear. They were saying that I busted his eardrum and I was going to jail. When the cops came they said that they weren't going to arrest me but they told my mom she had to bring me to school the next day for a conference in order for me to come back to the school. My mom was so fed up with my behavior that she didn't say anything to me when she picked me up from the school. I think the reason the school didn't pursue anything was because the teacher had no business throwing anything at a student. My mom took me back to the school on Monday they said I couldn't come back to the school and I had to go to 110 Livingston Street the Board of Education to have a hearing. My mom told me I was going to go Spofford Juvenile Detention Center especially after what the Judge told me from the last school incident I believed my mom. I couldn't go back to school until we had this hearing and I was on strict punishment. No T.V. no phone calls I couldn't even sit on the fire escape which I love doing whenever I was on punishment.

I shared a room with my sister and she was in school this day. I was at home waiting to go to my school hearing to determine what was going to happen to me. I was so afraid of getting sent away to kiddy jail. As I was laying across my bed I began to feel sad not knowing what was going to happen to me. I decided to kill myself. My sister had some pills because she use to cramp really bad during her monthly menstrual that time of the month. I will never forget the pills named pamprin. They were sitting on her night stand where she always kept her toiletries. My sister is five years older than I am so she had a lot of girly stuff on her night table. Her Perfume, lotion, and her makeup which she was allowed to wear and I wasn't. I opened the cap and poured some pills in my mouth I think I took like five pills. I remember just laying back on my bed waiting to die. My mom came into my room for whatever reason and saw the open pill bottle and started talking to me I don't remember what she was saying but I remember her standing over the bed. The ambulance came and took me to the hospital. The doctors kept asking me how many pills did I take but I really didn't know so I said five. They gave me some stuff to drink that tasted horrible because they wanted me to throw up whatever pills were in my stomach. I didn't really want to die, I just wanted to stop the hurt and pain I felt had consumed by young life. After discharging me they told my mom she have to take me to a psychiatrist since I tried to commit suicide. Let me just interject and say again "But God" only God could have allowed my mom to walk in that room at the exact moment I took those pills. When I say that God was covering and protecting me when I didn't even know it. I am truly and forever grateful for his grace and mercy. But for the grace of God I could have died but he found a purpose and a reason to spare my life so many more times as you will read. Let's continue on.

Chapter 10

Was I Crazy or Just Seeking Attention

My mom took me to a psychiatrist life she was advised to by the doctor. The doctor had referred her to a specialist who dealt with children. I had already decided that I wasn't saying jack to this doctor, specialist or psychiatrist and I would refused to talk. The psychiatrist kept showing me all kinds of pictures and asking me what did I see and I would just look at her like she was crazy. I totally refused to answer any of the questions I was asked. Then a man came into the room. I guess they figured I would talk to him. Little did they know he was old and reminded me of one of the men who molested me so I definitely wasn't saying anything too him. After several attempts to get mw to talk they realized that I wasn't going to be easily broken. What they didn't know was I was so use to hiding my feelings and covering up my pain that this was easy for me. I knew how to block you out like you weren't even there. And in my mind you weren't there. It was a defense mechanism for me. I didn't want to let anyone into my space unless I chose to. I remember the psychiatrist telling my mom I could return to school. They didn't find anything mentally wrong with me. I was just stubborn but they didn't know my mom was a part of my pain. I wanted her to protect me more, to display love as she had done to my sister and brothers. I felt like an outsider an outcast in my own family. I felt unloved and unwanted so I looked for love and acceptance in all the wrong place. Before I was allowed to return to school, my mom had to take me back to the Board of Education. Though they did not arrest me for the chair incident, I was suspended from the school pending a Chancellors Hearing at 110 Livingston Street. We went to the hearing and I had to give yet another sworn statement as to what happened that day. I did tell the truth or at my version of the truth. I did admit I had the chair in my hand but I never admitted ton trying to hit him with it. I said it was a reaction to him throwing the eraser at hitting me in the face with hit. That was an exaggeration because the eraser hit me on my shoulder nowhere near my face. My teacher wasn't at the hearing which I was kind of glad because if his ear was bandaged up it would have looked worse for me I thought. After the hearing was over the panel had me and my mom step out of the room while they made a determination of what to do with this problem child. The hearing board decided I would be yet again transferred to another Junior High School. Ok so how here is my third junior high school and I wasn't even out of the 6th grade. I was a little sad because I didn't know where or what school they were going to transfer me to. Of course my fears came true. Well to my dismay I was transferred to a School in Bay Ridge Brooklyn called Shallow J.H.S. I was upset that they decided to send me so far away to school. I   had never even heard of this school or Bay Ridge for that matter. I just knew it wasn't nowhere near my Flatbush neighborhood. I had already decided I was going to do something to get myself kicked out of this school. I hoped if I was bad enough they would return me to a school closer to my neighborhood. I will never forget my first day at this school. First of all, I had to take two trains. I was use to taking the train because I use to travel to the Bronx so that wasn't the problem. The school was about a block and a half from the train station. What shocked the heck out of me was all I saw were white kids. Tall ones, short ones, fat ones, skinny ones, all white kids. I was placed in a class and it seemed ok until I noticed my class had three black students and that included me. Out of 20 something kids in my class, there was 1 black boy and 1 black girl, I made 3. I soon found out there were eleven black students in the whole entire school. I couldn't believe this. This was unheard of. I came from a black school in a black neighborhood so this was heavy for me. I knew it would take some adjusting to. I was really determined to get the heck out of this school and this neighborhood for that matter. Well it only got worse. The students in Shallow JHS were VERY racist and the hand full of us black kids that were in the school had to literally run to the R. train every day. The white kids would chase us in cars and on foot. We were taunted with verbal insults and threats. They would curse at us and to make matters worse they threw sticks and bottles at us all the while telling us to get out of their neighborhood and calling us every nigger you could think of. What helped me a little bit was my red hair. They didn't know rather was I black or white or mixed but they still picked on me as well. We had to deal with this in the classroom as well. To tell you the truth I wasn't afraid to bring my knife for protection but I thought what would happen to me if I stabbed one of these kids. I did not want to go to jail for these white kids. They didn't know my background or my history but I knew I had to chill out in this school because this was my final warning. My two options were to do the right thing or end up in juvey jail. My two black classmates and I would sit together in class and in the lunchroom. This was our way of protecting each other and showing the other kids that we were going to stick together. The white kids would shoot spit ball through straws at us. They would put thumb tacks in our chair. Spit on our desk, rip up our books and the saddest of all was the teacher did nothing. All the black kids would sit in the lunch room together at one table. This was the only table we could sit at because all the white kids had all the rest of the tables. We were all experiencing the same abuse even the other black kids who were not in my class. We were so fed up that one day we met a couple of other black kids in the lunch room and we decided we weren't going to run that day. We made a pact that after school we were going to stand up to the white kids who were bullying us. It was either now or never. We had to take a stand or the rest of our school year was going to be torture. After school as we were walking out the school, they were waiting for us and one boy walked up to us and started to yell racist remarks in our faces. Well one young lady who was very tall and broad stood up to the white boy and told him we were not going to run anymore. Well he spit in her face and all hell broke loose. She grabbed him and commenced to beating the crap out of him and when his friends tried to jump in we stood our ground and would not allow anyone to jump in. We stood up to them and we would not back down. That day we won our respect and our liberty because we stood up for ourselves. The word that the black kids wasn't having it anymore must have gotten around the school because they did not follow us to the train or try to fight us ever again. That was the beginning of us enjoying school because we now had a reputation of not being afraid to fight back and the white kids started wanting to be our friend. I ended up graduating from that school and to this day I am still friends with many of my peers who went to that school.

Chapter 11

Feeling Lonely

I was missing my boyfriend in the Bronx and I felt the need to go visit him. I started sneaking to the Bronx every chance I got. I would lie and tell my mom I was going to visit a friend then I would get on the train and go to the Bronx. The train ride was about an hour from my house so it wasn't a long ride. I would spend a couple of hours then take the train back home. I got away with sneaking to the Bronx because I would come back at a reasonable time. I didn't over do it because I sure did not want my mom to get wind of what I was doing. Once the summer came back around I begged my mom to go back to the Bronx. I finally graduated out of the junior high school so mom was happy with me. I had another best friend who I grew up with In Brooklyn but her family moved to the Bronx. We lived on the same block where our friend got killed by her boyfriend on East 19th street. My mom would allow me to go spend weekends and weeks at a time in the summer at her house as well. I guess my mom felt it was better to allow me to go to the Bronx instead of worrying about what kind of trouble I would get into if I was at home. Knowing me and my rebellious way, I would have found some trouble to get into. Trouble was always easy to get into but as I continued to learn hard to get out. The fun things about being in the Bronx was my best friends mom worked at night. We would put on our pajamas and act like we were going to bed and as soon as she left for work we would put on our clothes and hit the street. There was always a schoolyard jam or a D.J. battle which as I explained before was two

DJ'S would set up their music equipment and I am talking about real turntables and 3 feet tall huge speakers not like today where they play CD'S but this was the real deal. The Dee jays would set their music up across from each other and try and pull the crowd to their side of the school yard while blasting the latest jams that would make you dance till sweat poured off your face. Life was grand then, you didn't have to worry too much about gang shootings or shooting up the party. People settled their beef with their fist not guns and knives. I mean we had our share of violence but it wasn't as bad as it is today. We would break day at these schoolyard jams sometimes they would end at wee hours in the morning. We just had to be in the bed before her mom got home from work. I remember one time we could not wake up her sister or brother to get in the house so we had to climb up the fire escape. Luckily she only lived on the second floor. During the day we would go to Sedgwick Avenue to hang out with my boyfriend. I knew he was way too old for me But I didn't care I liked having an older man taking care of me, putting money in my pockets and giving me all the free weed I wanted. I knew eventually I would have to sleep with him. I was a semi-virgin meaning I had been touched and tampered with but no real action. I had one episode with an older guy already but I really didn't count that because he just used me and played with my feelings. I had a close school that I use to hang out with when I went to Walt Whitman. She use to go with my brother Steven. She had a cousin that was the finest thing since Billy Dee back in those days. I was so in like with my friends cousin. He was living with them at that time. This was before I got kicked out of Walt Whitman. He claimed he liked me as well. I was a virgin and he knew it. He use to tell me how beautiful I was and I guess I needed to hear that and feel wanted. I use to go spend the night at their house and he lived upstairs on the second floor. It was a private house that her family owned. Her and I would go upstairs and hang out with him and he would smoke weed. One weekend when I was over there I went upstairs to hang out with him by myself. He started kissing me and being that I liked him I was all for it. Before you know it we were humping with our clothes still on, the problem was I had no experience at all. So he took control and advantage of me but I was willing as well. We ended up going all the way and I started crying because it was very painful. He stopped after realizing I wasn't as mature as I to act like I was. When he turned on the light there was blood all over the bed. I didn't even know I was bleeding. That's when I learned when you first have actual intercourse you bleed. I was scared and I remember he was laughing and I didn't see anything funny. When I told his cousin what happened she told everybody in school and I wanted to fight her. We didn't talk for a while but eventually we made up. When I went back to her house her cousin treated me as though nothing between him and I never happened. I was hurt but I came to find out that he had a girlfriend. I was hurt because he took my virginity and it didn't mean nothing to him. Well I knew I wasn't going to ever tell my new boyfriend about that as far as he knew I was still a virgin, and that was how it was going to stay. I knew eventually I was going to have sex with my Bronx boyfriend. I was kind of ready because he was so good to me. He wasn't rushing me into doing it but he would hint around to it. We did a lot of kissing and breast touching but whenever it got to heavy I would tell him I wasn't ready. Plus we were rarely alone because he shared the apartment/weed spot with his partner. To top it all off because it was a weed spot the doorbell constantly rang. There was never a full 10 minutes that someone wasn't at the door. We would be in his room with the door closed while his friend would hold it down but most of the time they took turns answering the door or as they called it they had shifts. I remember my first time having sex with my old man boyfriend. I really liked him mainly because he was a very nice person. He had a big heart and was very caring. Though I knew he was too old for me I loved the fact that he treated me so nice. I felt I was ready to sleep with him it had already been about a year since I first met him. I knew I was already to give him some. My only problem was having sex inside of this spot He was living in. There was just entirely no alone time or privacy. I remember the special knock the customers us to use, he would go to the door, drop the cylinder lock out which was attached to a string and the buyer would pass the money through the hole. He would then pass the weed back through the hole. He sold tray bags for $ 3.00 nickel bags $5.00 and dime bags for $10.00. He made plenty of money because he was the only weed spot in the area. Back then there was not much completion so he didn't have nobody trying to steal his customers. He taught me how to bag up the weed and I started helping him sell it so he would hit me off with more money for selling weed for him. He would leave the apartment for hours at a time and leave me in there to sell the weed for him. He trusted me and I was on easy street. Selling and smoking as much weed as I wanted to it was always at my disposal. I didn't realize how illegal. I mean I knew it wasn't legal but I figured he had it made and no one was going to rat them put. I mean the whole building was coming down there buying weed even the superintendent of the building. I thought it was cool they didn't seem afraid to live in the house that they was selling the weed from. My summers were so much fun because I knew I would get to spend them with my boyfriend. When school started back I didn't want to go to school because I wanted to stay in the Bronx with my man and I mean that literally because he was a man after all he was 8 years older than me.

Chapter 12

Being Accepted

I was now attending Eramus Hall High School I made it to High School which no one through I would heck even I didn't see high school in my future. After going to 3 different junior high schools I really didn't want to see another school again. Once I got into Eramus, I was happy because all my of friends from Walt Whitman went there so we were all back together again. In high school it was so easy to cut class. All I had to do was show up in homeroom sign in for attendance then I would leave the school and go to the Bronx. I had gotten so use to being up there for the summer that when I was away from him I would miss him. So it was easy for me to just make a decision to go be with him every chance I got. I knew I was ready to sleep with him and I decided it was time. I cut school and snuck to the Bronx I called myself surprising him. Well I got the surprise he had another girl in the weed spot. Well, this was the first time he saw me lose my cool. I wanted to fight her. I was uncontrollable. I don't know why I wanted to fight her she didn't know me. I should have been fighting him because he was cheating on me not her. He made her leave and told me how sorry he was. I knew then I had to step up my game and sleep with him because he was seeing other females. That same day after I cried and he comforted me I told him I was ready to go to have sex with him. He asked me if I was sure I wanted to do it. Of course I knew if I wanted to keep him I had to up the panties. He was so gentle with me and made me feel like a real woman would feel. I feel instantly more in love with him. Though it wasn't really my first time but it was the best time I had with a man. I was willing this wasn't forced or against my will and he was so caring with me. He thought he was my first and I decided to leave it that way. He made the most sweet passionate love to me and he introduced me to stuff I never knew could feel so good. I left the Bronx that afternoon to go home with the biggest smile on my face. I had money in my pocket. I had plenty of weed and I finally slept with my boyfriend. I felt like a million bucks. I was cutting school so much that eventually the school called my mom. As a freshman it wasn't a good way to start the school year. My sister was in Eramus as well and she was an A student. I on the other hand had no interest in school. My sister was also a co-op student where she worked a week and went to school a week. Only exceptionally smart students got that privilege which my sister was. My mom came home from work that day and she confronted me about the school calling her. I told my mom they were lying on me and I do go to school. They decided to give me an attendance card and I had to have each teacher sign the card on a daily bases. Of course I knew how to get around that I would forge my teachers names and forge my mother's signature. I was getting away with it for a while until I forged one of my teacher name who wasn't in school that day and the next day when I went to turn in my attendance card to the homeroom teacher he busted me. When my mom found out I was forging her signature she put me on punishment. For me punishment didn't mean anything. All I couldn't do was go outside or talk on the phone but I knew the next time I got out the house I was going to do everything I wanted to do. I knew I had to sneak to the Bronx on the weekday because I would not be able to go on the weekend. At school I was put on academic probation like I really cared. I did decide it was time to change a little bit and sneak to the Bronx twice a week instead of everyday. The next day I snuck to the Bronx that morning instead of going to school. I figured they were watching me in school so it didn't make any since to go to school and cut classes so I just didn't go. When I got to the Bronx I had a funny feeling like something was wrong. I wasn't in tune with my spirituality so I really didn't know how to pick up on my feelings. I say this because when you are being led by God the Holy Spirit quickens your spirit: meaning you have a spirit of discernment you will be able to feel when something or someone isn't right in your spirit. I went to the weed spot/slash my boyfriend's house that morning. We made passionate love all morning. After we were done we were chilling watching a movie. I was about to get ready to go home and we heard all this loud noise outside. The cat ran under the bed so my boyfriend got up from the bed to see what was going on. He ran back into the room and said get dressed. I could tell something was wrong. I'm asking him what's going on as I am getting dressed. I saw how frantic and he just ignored me. He picked up the box that he kept the weed in and ran into the bathroom. I learn later to flush the weed down the toilet. I heard the front door being banged. Loud Booms!!! One after the other. It sounded like someone was running into the door with a car at full speed. The cops had a battering ram trying to knock the door down. I didn't know what a battering ram was until that day. The police took the entire door down and stormed the apartment with guns pointing at us yelling "get on the floor". I was in total shock afraid, scared, nervous I didn't know what was going on. I mean I wasn't dumb I knew we were being busted but I never thought I would be in this type of situation in my life. The police put some plastic cuffs on my wrist and made me sit on the floor with my boyfriend and his partner. They searched the whole entire apartment turning over furniture, cutting holes in the sofas, pulled all the food out the cabinets, opened all the unopen boxes that were in the cabinets, searched the closets, I mean I never seen anything like this before. They were on a mission to find anything and everything they came looking for. They took me out first after asking me my name and if I had any identification on me. All I had was my Eramus Hall high school Identification on me which turned out to be a blessing in disguise because I was a minor still in high school. When they walked me out in handcuffs the whole building and block was outside watching. I don't think I ever been so embarrassed in my whole life. This wasn't the first time I had been in handcuffs but it was the first time I had audience watching me. Once they got me to the precinct they started asking me a thousand questions trying to scare me into telling them what was going on in the weed spot. Well little did they know I had a lot of experience with being in trouble I knew I wasn't going to tell on my man. I knew because I was a minor they could not hold me but for so long without calling my mom. Well that was the problem because my mom did not know I cut school that day and now I am in the precinct all the way in the Bronx. After calling my mom they said I had to wait for someone to come get me from the precinct. Finally my uncles came to the precinct to get me and they were very upset. I lied and told them I had just got to the Bronx when they busted the spot but I had been there since morning. When I got home I guess my mom was just too through with me because she took away my keys. She really didn't speak to me which was worse because I did not know what she was thinking or going to do. The next day I went to school and decided I better stay in school all day because I was too afraid to go back up to the weed spot. I also was afraid that my mom was going to be checking up on me so I decided to play it safe. I was very concerned as to what happened to my boyfriend because the cops didn't tell me anything of course. I still had my beeper which he paid the bill for so I figured he would get in touch with me if anything. About 3 days passed and finally he beeped me. My mom had a lock on the kitchen phone so I could not sneak in there to call him back so I had to wait until the next day and hope he would beep me again. I didn't get any sleep that night I remember anticipating the next day hoping he would beep me again. Finally when I was in school he beeped me again and I asked for a bathroom pass. Once I got the pass I ran out of class to call him back. He answered and told me they found the weed he flushed down the toilet and he had guns in the weed spot. I never knew there were guns in the apartment. I'm glad I didn't know because I would have been scared. I hate guns and to this very day I hate guns. The guy he worked for bailed him out and he had to go back to court at a later date. He said told me that the charges were serious. He told me he would probably get some time in jail because this wasn't the first time he had a drug charge. I started crying. I was hurt because I finally found someone who I loved and now he had to go to hail. He asked me to come see him, but I had to tell him everything that happened with me and my uncles came to get me and I was on strict punishment. I couldn't even use the house phone and my mom took my keys from me. That weekend when my mom went to work I decided I wanted to see him, so on Saturday I got up got dressed and told my sister I was running away from home. I don't think she believed me because she never said a word. I guess I was just testing her. I wanted to see what she would say or would she tell my mom when she came home. I called her bluff. Well I decided that I would wait until Monday when I went to school that way everyone would just think I was in school.

Chapter 13

I Ran Away from Home

My mom never said anything to me when she came home. I assumed my sister never mentioned anything to her. On Monday I took my book bag and put some extra clothes in it knowing I was not coming back home. I left the house and decided it was best to go to home room and sign my name on the attendance sheet just in case my mom or the attendance office checked up on me. I left school with the Bronx as my destination. I had not spoken to my boyfriend being that I could not go outside or answer his pages on my beeper. My mom had not taken the lock off the kitchen phone because she knew I would sneak in the kitchen and use it, so I was going to the Bronx blindly hoping that he would be back in the spot which again doubled as his apartment. I had not been up there since the raid so I really didn't know if he was still there. I got to the Bronx and the block was extra quiet which was usual for Sedgwick Avenue even as early as it was it was normally a busy block. I went to the building and the people who knew me just looked like they were surprised to see me. I guessed it was because this was there first time seeing me since I came out in handcuffs so they didn't know what to say to me. By now they knew I was a little firecracker they had seen me spaz out a couple of times so they didn't say much to me. I went to the door and there was a huge chain on the door with a padlock and a DO NOT ENTER SIGN ON THE DOOR FROM THE City of New York. I am like oh no where is he. Then I heard someone call my name from in the hallway from up on the second floor. The weed spot was on the first floor. When I started going up the stairs it was his homeboy girlfriend. She told me they were using another apartment until they could move. So I went to the other apartment on the third floor and he was there. I was so happy to see him and he was happy to see me as well. I told him all about my mom locking up the phone and why I wasn't answering his beeps. He told me he tried to call me on my house phone but people kept hanging up on him when he would ask for me. My family didn't officially know him but they knew of him. I also found out that my mom's friend from the next building, who we were friends with their family since forever. It was her house I was staying in that summer when I first met my man. She had been asking questions about him. People told him she was asking about him. I figured my mom was trying to find out information on him. When I got arrested they did not really release any information about him to my uncles so no one really knew much about him but I was sneaking and breaking all the rules to be with him. I told him I didn't want to go back home and I was running away because I wanted to be with him and to my surprise he was all for it. He said he was staying in this other apartment but he will get something for us. I told I didn't want to stay in anymore drug spots. He was still selling weed and business had picked up because there a new kind of weed was out called 'SNUCK". I guess it got that name because it was powerful and smelled very strong. I was happy to try this new weed I came at the right time. That night we went to stay in another apartment across town but still in the Bronx. His friend was renting this apartment for him because he didn't want anything in his name being that he still had an open court case from the weed bust. I liked this apartment it was fully furnished and it was in a nice area. It was in a very quiet area and you had to ring the bell in order to get in the building. Unlike the other spot where the door was open to the building 24/7. I met his little friend Malik this young boy I mean I was young to but he was younger then I was. I felt like I was grown now since I was sexually active, smoking weed, got arrested twice, stabbed someone, got kicked out of 2 schools and ran away from home so you couldn't tell me I wasn't grown. Malik and I hit it off well he liked me instantly I guess because we were in the same age range. I had been in the Bronx for 2 days and I was happy not being home. My childhood friend who I met him through came over to the new apartment. I was kind of confused as to how she knew where he lived at. Well my boyfriend had left to go sell his week in the old neighborhood and he left Her, Malik and myself in the apartment. He gave me some money to feed us and left us some weed. She started telling me how my mom was looking for me and that they said I ran away from home. She promised she would not tell that she knew where I was. Malik kept giving her dirty looks and noticed he was being rude to her. I told him her and I grew up together as childhood friends. Now Malik was so cute he was mixed black/Hispanic with shoulder length hair. He asked me if I knew how to braid which of course I did. So as I was braiding his hair the three of us were laughing and talking, I noticed he had gotten very quiet. After we smoked some weed and drank a 40oz of beer he loosened up and said very bluntly. I'm only telling you this because I really like you and you seem nice. She was over here the other day with fino and they had sex. I almost choked on my saliva. I could not believe what he just said to me, on top of that she was sitting there and he said it right in her face. Of course she denied it and I started yelling asking her was this true. She kept saying he was lying and he just liked her. They started arguing and she tried to jump in his face but for some reason I knew he tell was not lying he was swearing on ever body and they momma that he was telling the truth. It just so happened that there was a Bible in the house and he went and got the Bible and put his hand on it and swore that he was not lying so I told her to put her hand on the bible she wouldn't do it, so I grabbed her by her hair and commenced to beating the crap out of her and he jumped in and we beat her up something terrible. I was hurt beyond words and could not believe that either one of them would do this to me. We threw her out of the apartment and I waited ranting and raving about what I was going to do to him when he came back. I cried so hard because this was my first real true love and I could not believe this was happening to me. I felt like I turned my back on my momma failed in school got arrested and all this for a man who slept with one of my best friends. I mean this deep for me. She was more than a friend. Our families had been friends literally since I could remember my whole young life. I told Malik to leave because I did not want my boyfriend to do anything to him for telling me but he wanted to stay just in case my boyfriend tried to do something to hurt me. I was almost tempted to sleep with Malik at that very moment just because I was so angry and I wanted to pay my boyfriend back, but I was too angry and hurt to get in any sexual mood. We smoked all my boyfriends weed I was so mad I did not care I just wanted to medicate my pain. Finally after waiting hours which seemed like forever my boyfriend came with food for me and a big smile on his face. When I heard his key in the door I prepared myself to just attack him and scratch his face up. One thing I could do was fight I had a lot of experience with that. When he came in he saw my face which had a look like "negro please don't say nothing to me". He asked what was wrong and I got up off of the couch and stepped in his face. I asked how could you do this to me I started swinging on him, he was trying to hold my arms to keep me from hitting him in his face which was what I was aiming for. I was swinging, crying, screaming, cursing all at one time and he is now asking Malik what happened and Malik said she know about you and Renee. He started screaming at Malik and I told him don't blame him you the one who cheated on me with my best friend. I'm still hitting him and cursing and Malik is now trying to hold me because I was totally out of control. One thing I can honestly say is not one time did my boyfriend try to hit me back or hurt me he was just trying to keep me from hurting him or myself. I was like a caged lion who just got free. He at one point grabbed me and held me and I just cried on his chest like why did you do this to me. Why did you hurt me like this? What did she have that I didn't have? Was she better in bed then I was? So many questions where racing through my head and all I could do cry. He told Malik to leave and gave him money to take a cab home. After Malik left he first tried to lie and say it didn't happen, but after I told him how I beat her up he then tried to blame it all on her. I wasn't falling for it because you had to bring her here to the apartment in order for her to know where it was. I told him I was going back home and I didn't want anything to do with him anymore but deep down inside I knew I didn't mean it I just wanted to make him think I was breaking up with him. He begged me not to go he, told me how sorry he, and that he would never hurt me again but I wasn't hearing any of it. He went in his pocket and gave me a couple of hundred dollars because he knew how to buy my love and I happily took the money but I did not let him know I was happy. He told me he was going to take me shopping the next day if I didn't leave. I really did not want to go home anyway I kind of like the fact that I ran away and no one knew where I was. Or so I thought. This chick not only slept with my man but she told her mom where I was who in turn told my mom where I was. Unbeknownst to me, my mom sent my brothers and cousin to the Bronx to get me next day. Here is how it unfolded: My boyfriend went to work on Sedgwick Avenue to sell his weed. I decided to go hang out with him and his friends at the weed spot. I also had friends on the block on since I was over there so much, Plus I wanted that chick to see him and I were still together and even though she slept with him I wasn't going nowhere. There was going to be a party that night and I was looking forward to going. My boyfriend's homeboy was having a house party and everybody and their momma was going to be there. House parties back then were different because people would take all the furniture and put it in one room and have a real DJ come rock the house. Normally you paid a door cover charge like $5 but I wouldn't pay because my man had juice so I had juice as well. My boyfriend took me shopping to buy new clothes and a special outfit for the party. He was still making up for cheating on me. We decided to dress alike and I was excited about this because I felt like everyone would really know now I was his main chick. He was the most popular drug dealer in the hood and I was his lady so I had my props from everybody. That night we were getting for the party, he was in the weed spot on the first floor. The spot still had a huge chain and padlock on the door. The Do Not Enter by order of the Police Department" was still on the door. They found a way to enter through the fire escape and still sell weed out of the spot. The good thing was the cops would not have known the spot was still being used because the chain and padlock were still on the door. The super was too afraid to rat them out to the police. First of all, he was scared to go against the drug dealers he had to live there with his family plus he was being paid very lovely to keep his mouth shut. The good thing for me was I wasn't allow back into the spot because they had to climb in and out of the window so my boyfriend didn't want me in there. The door was still used for the main source of selling the weed by dropping out the peephole and passing the money through and the product would be passed back through the hole. They stopped using the cylinder because the cops was hip to it. I started hanging upstairs at my friend's house. I still didn't want anything to do with my childhood friend after she slept with my man but funny how I forgave him but not her. That night we were at my friend's house getting ready for the party which was in the next building. I was waiting for her to get dressed and everyone started coming to tell us there was a group of guys at the party asking for me and my man. They knew his name because of my friend and her big mouth. As I went to the building I see my brother and cousin standing there. I'm like oh hell no this is not real. I see my boyfriend's friend standing at the top of the stairs like he was ready to fight. This Negro had on a black ninja suit on with the black Chinese slippers. He had a pair of chucks in his hand and he was swinging them around this neck and over his head. I didn't know rather to laugh or cry because to see him standing there looking like a black Bruce Lee was hilarious. A crowd had gathered and he was telling my brother and cousin if they come up the stairs he was going to kick their butts. Well my brother who was known to always carry a gun, pulls out his gun and tells the friend "by the time you jump down the stairs he is going to put a bullet in him". I'm standing here looking in complete shock at all that is transpiring. My man now comes up the stairs and he's asking what's going on. My cousin sees him and automatically recognize him. Come to find out they went to High School together. How ironic is this my boyfriend is from the Bronx and my cousin is from Brooklyn but they went to the same high school. Well come to find out my boyfriend was originally from Brooklyn. He grew up in Bush Wick. My cousin and my man went to Thomas Jefferson High School and knew each other very well. They were good friends in High School. The good thing was it calmed the situation down and there was no violence. Every one calmed down and the tension ceased but the bad thing was my mom sent them up there to bring me home. I didn't want to go back home but I knew I had no choice. We stayed a little bit at the party but eventually we left and headed back to Brooklyn. When we got home it was wee hours in the morning and my mom who was working the grave yard shift at the time was not home. I knew that morning I would have to deal with her for running away. I had been gone for like a week and I found out they called the cops and filed a missing person's report. When my mom found out I was dating a man 8 years older than she decided to press charges against him for statuary rape for dating a minor. My mom took me to court to file charges against my man. I remember going before a judge in family court. I was asked if I was sexually active with him I told them no we never had sex that I just liked him. I hated lying because he was my man and I was proud of it but I didn't want to get him in any trouble plus he already had to go back to court for the drug charges. Since I wouldn't admit to being sexually active with him they had no case against him. I remember my mom threatening me saying if I go back to the Bronx she is going to have me put away in a group home. I didn't want to go to a group home I knew a lot about girl's homes and I didn't want to end up in one. My cousin and my bother both had girlfriends that lived in a group home. I use to go hang out at the group home on Ocean Avenue where their girlfriends lived. This home allowed visitors to come spend time during the day. They had to ask for permission just to go outside. They had to sign in and out as they leave or enter the premises. They sat down at a certain time to eat breakfast lunch and dinner. They had no freedom. No phones in their rooms only a main house phone which everyone used. They had to share everything as far as their stationary and sanitary items. They wore each other clothes and they fought over everything. I did not want to have to live like that. My home life wasn't that bad when I thought about it. I shared a room with my sister and I got to wear her nice clothes. Half the time she didn't know I had on her clothes so I had to sneak and put them back before she found out I wore them. She brought a lot of her own clothes because she worked. I had a lot of nice clothes to but most of my name brand stuff was in the Bronx. I couldn't bring them home and let my mom see them. She didn't buy them so she would have known they came from my boyfriend. I sure didn't have a job to buy new clothes.

Chapter 14

I'm Gonna Try to Shape Up

I really didn't want to end up in a home so I decided it was time to shape up. Especially after my boyfriend cheated on me I realized I was chasing behind someone who wasn't taking me as serious as I was taking him. Plus I felt I am still young I could have any boyfriend I want I didn't need no man in his twenties and I was still a teenager. I went to school the next couple of weeks and my grades picked up. I finished the tenth grade to my surprise and was really proud of myself. My mom was happy as well because my grades were improving. I decided I wanted to at least get out of High School. Running to the Bronx was not helping me get my education. That summer I decided to stay home and hang out on my block. I had missed out on being a teenager and hanging with my friends. I was so busy running behind this man. Most of my friends smoked weed so I was smoking daily and now drinking beer. We had our click that hung out together every day. At least I was now home not running to the Bronx. During the summer months I began to feel sick in the mornings. I would wake up feeling nausea and light headed. I didn't tell my mom because I didn't want her to worry or take me to the doctor. I missed my period for a month but I didn't think much of it. I would tell my friends that I woke up sick and they told me to buy a pregnancy test. I beeped my boyfriend who I hadn't seen in a while. I was ok with that because I was still hurt about him cheating on me even though I forgave him I was still hurt over it. He called back the payphone I beeped him from and I told him what was going on with me and he told me to buy a pregnancy test and let him know the results. I told him I needed some money because the money he gave me a couple of weeks ago was getting low. He said I could come get it but I did not want to go to the Bronx so I told him I would meet him half way on the train. He agreed to meet me at 42nd street. I got on the train that day and met him on 42nd street. I was really happy to see him though I tried to act like I wasn't. We decided to grab a bite to eat since we were in already in Manhattan. After we ate it was getting late I knew I needed to get home. I was trying to be on my best behavior with mom watching my every move. I told him I would let him know what happened after I took the pregnancy test. The next day I went and brought the pregnancy test. I nervous to take it. I felt like I was pregnant. I had never been pregnant but I had friends who were and they told me I had the same symptoms they had when they first got pregnant. Not that I was surprised when the test came back positive that I was pregnant. I was in shock that it was confirmed. Now what do I do? Here I am pregnant and I didn't have a clue as to what to do. I beeped my man immediately and told him I was pregnant. He sounded just as shocked as I was. He was quiet for a few seconds then he asked me what do you want to do? He didn't have any children and neither did I. I asked him what did he want me to do and he said to have it he will take care of me and the baby. I believed that part because he already took very good care of me financially. I knew me or my baby wouldn't want for anything. I told him we needed to talk in person and he should come to Brooklyn. He didn't want to come to Brooklyn, he knew my family didn't approve of him and I being together, but to me this was different. We now have a baby Involved. He told me he wanted to see me first so we could talk. I decided to go spend the day with him so we could talk. I woke up Saturday morning and told my mom I was going to the Bronx for the day. I promised I would come home, well to my surprise she let me go without any argument. I guess she figured I would sneak and go anyway so she might as well agree to let me go. At least I was honest and told her where I would be that day which normally I would've just went and not cared how she felt. I knew my attitude was changing and I kind of liked it. I needed to be responsible and mature if I was going to become a mother. I beeped him and he answered right back. I told him I was on my way up there and he said he was at his house not at the drug spot. He picked me up from the train station and we went to his house. He asked me if I was hungry which he always made sure I had food in my stomach. We started talking and I told him I needed him to be honest and tell me if he really wanted me to have his baby. He started telling me that he wanted me to keep the baby and I started crying tears of joy. He said I needed to go to the doctor and find out how many months I was. I knew I was at least a month because I missed a period. He wanted me to take a pregnancy test where he could see the results so we went to the drug store and he brought a test. I know for sure I was pregnant but I did it to let him see I wasn't lying. When we got back I kept drinking water until I had to pee. I took the test and he saw for himself that it came back positive. He picked me up in his arms and we kissed until we started making love. After that we talked and ate more food and made love again. It was dark by now so I decided to head home before it got so late. He gave me a couple hundred dollars and walked me to the train. I was so happy because he wanted the baby. My first child and the father was a big baller drug dealer making mad money and he didn't have any kids. So my child would be the apple of his eye. Now I the drama began. I had to figure out how I was going to break this news to my mom. I knew she was going to hit every ceiling in the house and probably put me out. We did not have any room for a baby. My sister and I already shared a room which was tight as it was. I knew she would not take this news lightly, I decided not to say anything until I went to the doctor and found out for sure that I was pregnant. One of my best friends who was pregnant as well told me to go to Planned Parenthood and speak to a counselor. They do not inform your parent and they help you make the right decision that's best for you. I told my boyfriend about it and he agreed I should go there. I went to the one Downtown Brooklyn on Court Street and to my surprise they took me as a walk in. after speaking to someone and getting a counselor they made arrangements for me to have a pregnancy test. They took my blood and urine and told me they would have the results in48 hours I guess it had to go to the lab. I went back to Planned Parenthood in two days and just as I had suspected I was pregnant. They did an exam and I was about 8 weeks pregnant which was more than I thought. They asked me what I wanted to do and I said I wanted to keep my baby. They asked me did the child father know I was pregnant and I told them yes but I could not give them any information because he was way older than I was plus I thought about when my mom tried to get him locked up. I didn't know what would happen if I told them how old he was. Now that I was 100 percent sure I was pregnant, I had a lot of decisions to make. The first one was did I really want to be a mother. I figured I had nothing to lose because I had nothing anyway. I already felt like I was the black sheep in the family.

Chapter 15

Why Am I the Black Sheep

Most of the time I felt unloved and unwanted by my mom. I wasn't always the easiest child to get alone with but that was because of all I went through growing up. I always felt so alone like no one cared. In my eyes that was truly the case no one didn't care. Now I am pregnant and I didn't care if they liked it or not. I finally would have something of my own. My own possession. My own child. Someone who would love me in spite of me. I knew I was not going to tell my mom right away, especially after the lady told me I had up to 5 months to have an abortion. I decided to wait and think about what I really wanted to do. The morning sickness increased, there were days I felt like I just didn't want to be pregnant anymore. Summer was over and I was back in school. I was now in the 11th grade and really proud of myself. My pregnancy wasn't really showing yet so I was able to get by without anyone thinking I was pregnant. One day my mom asked me why wasn't I using any sanitary napkins. I told her I had my own in my room that I got from school. The school did have some in the nurse office but of course that was not true. Months passed and I started showing probably by 4 months. One day my mom asked me was I pregnant because my face had gotten fat and I looked round in the belly. Of course I totally denied it. Knowing that I would have to fess up eventually and tell her the truth. I was really waiting until it was too late for me to have an abortion. That way she couldn't force me to kill my baby. My best friend was pregnant and I wanted to be a mother like her. One day I was really feeling the morning sickness, so I decided not to go to school. My mom was home because she worked overnight. She kept asking me why I wasn't going to school. I told her I did not feel well. She said you think I'm stupid or something I know you're pregnant. You haven't used a pad in months and I notice you look round in the stomach. My mom threatened to take me to The GYN doctor so I finally admitted to her that I was pregnant. Needless to say she was furious I had just turned 16 in July and I was due to give birth in October. I told her I went to the doctor 2 months ago and they told me I was pregnant. She called me every name in the book and told me I was not bringing no baby in her house I wasn't responsible enough to have a baby. I told her I was keeping my baby and I would go live in the Bronx with my boyfriend. She said she wanted to meet him that he need to come to the house and sit down and talk to her about what we were going to do. I already knew I was going to keep my baby so I did not care what she talked to him about. Neither one of them could change my mind plus I felt the baby move a couple of times. I was so excited about feeling a life moving inside of me. It is a feeling you can't explain. The next few days were tense because my mom was not speaking to me. The whole family now knew I was pregnant. My siblings weren't too happy, mind you both of my brothers had children already but no one was mad at them. I guess because I was the black sheep it made things even worse for me. I started going to the Bronx again and that was mainly because my baby father was treating me like a queen waiting on me hand and foot. He gave me anything and everything I asked for. I told him my mom wanted him to come to Brooklyn. He wasn't too happy about it but he knew he would have to face her eventually. I remember when he first came to my house being that just about everybody in my house except my sister smoked weed, I suggested he bring some weed with him and that would break the ice. He came to Brooklyn on a Friday and to my surprise everybody was nice to him. My cousin and brother already knew him from when they came to the Bronx to get me several months ago. My mom wasn't as mean to him as I thought she would be. They actually liked him. I can say he was really a nice person. He was very mild mannered. He rarely raised his voice. He never put his hands on me no matter how many times I would swing on him he would just hold me and try to calm me down. I had a lot of anger issues and it didn't take nothing but a second for me to snap. He gave everybody weed including my mom so now he was really in there with the family. We talked that night him, my mom, my stepdad and I.

He told my mom he would take care of the baby and buy me the things I would need. My mom already knew he was a weed dealer. She didn't like it but I think she was comfortable knowing the baby would be provided for as long. He left that night and said he would come back tomorrow and see me and hang out with my family. I was ok with that because now we were no longer boyfriend and girlfriend but we were now going to be parents of a child. The next day he came back and hung out with my brothers and cousins. My stepdad was the super of the building we lived in. We had full access to the basement which we used to have parties on the weekends. My brother use to have DJ equipment actually he still to this day play music and we use to have jams in the basement. Our parties were the place to be we had the red and blue flashing lights. The basement was lit with weed you would catch a contact just walking in the door. People brought their own weed to smoke and you could bring your own brown bag. My boyfriend fit right in because he sold weed so he made money at the parties. Now everybody really liked him I was happy about that. My pregnancy was showing now. It felt Funny carrying this extra weight in front of me. I was use to wearing my tight clothes, form fitting jeans showing off my cute figure but now he had to buy me maternity clothes. I didn't like maternity clothes they made me feel like an old lady but they were comfortable and the proper clothing for my belly. The pants had elastic waist bands so they were really comfortable. I felt like and official expectant mother with my maternity gear. A lot of people in my neighborhood was surprised to see me pregnant first of all I was young and they never seen me with a boyfriend but that was because he lived in the Bronx. Around my fifth month of pregnancy I was turning 16years old and my boyfriend decided finally he wanted me to meet his family. I was happy about that because I never met anyone in his family since I met him almost two years ago.

Chapter 16

Finally Feeling Loved

I remember he first took me to Queens where his grandparents own their own home. I didn't know any people that owned a house so I was impressed. I met his grandparents they were very nice to me. I met his sister and her daughter. He also had a cousin who lived there as well we hit it off instantly. She was cool and down to earth and she had a big beautiful heart. She was obese but she was so beautiful on the inside that her size didn't matter. She had such high self-confidence and I loved it. She made me see myself as beautiful. That helped me a lot being that I suffered with self-esteem issues because of all I had been through growing up. I loved his grandparents they were so loving and kind to me. They were a taken aback at how young I was, I could tell they didn't approve of my being so young and pregnant, but it was too late for anyone to tell me what to do I was showing and proud of my belly. That night it got late so we stayed over in queens. I slept downstairs in his sister room with her and her daughter and he slept upstairs in the living room. I loved being in queens it was so different than being in Brooklyn, the streets were quiet and clean and people were friendly. We sat outside on the porch as they told me their childhood stories. I didn't share much because my childhood wasn't always a happy one. What was I going to tell them about oh by the way I was molested most of my young life by my mom boyfriends. Nope, don't think that would not have been a good topic. I just enjoyed hearing their stories. I got to meet a lot of his friends who came to the house when they heard he was in the neighborhood. On friend stuck out to me there was something about him I did not like. He seemed to be a sneaky person. I later found out why I didn't like him. He had a girlfriend and they had a daughter together. This guy was his best friend they grew up together. I wondered why if he was his best friend why I never met in to two years of knowing my man. I would soon find out why. We went to their house and her mother and sister lived with them. He was very abusive to her mother. He would call her all kinds of names and his girlfriend would sit there and allow him to disrespect her mom. Now let me just say, my mom and I didn't have the best relationship but let someone try and disrespect my momma especially in my face and they would have a problem. One time we were over their house and I watched him beat up his girlfriend. I could not believe what I was seeing. She was in the corner on the floor in a fetal position and he was wailing on her like she was a man. Her mom tried to stop him and he took the back of his hand and slapped her mom across the face like she was a rag doll. My boyfriend finally grabbed him and took him outside. I just sat there in shock at what I had just seen. I knew this was something that always happened because the sister didn't even come out of her room. I was mad and disgusted at what I had just seen. I was new to this domestic violence stuff, my answer was to get a knife and stab him. She was petrified of him it showed all over her face. We left that night and I told my man that I did not like his friend. He told me they grew up together in Bush wick and knew each other since they were kids. I still didn't like him though. A few days later he took me to bush wick where his mom and brothers lived. I met his mother and stepfather who seemed cool. As always everyone wanted to know how old I was and I didn't mind telling them I was 16. His brother and his wife and lived upstairs in the same house as his mom. I loved being over there, being in a house was much different than being in an apartment. They all seemed to like me though they were surprised at how young I was. He had a brother who was gay and I just loved him. He made me laugh watching his mannerisms. His other brothers didn't like the way he was acting around the kids. The fact that he had on hot pinks shorts and a cut off shirt didn't help either. They were having a birthday party for this brother son who was turning three. The brother told the gay brother that he didn't appreciate him coming to his house dressed like that. The gay brother got upset and left. I was upset that he left because I liked him. My man had 4 brothers and 1 sister. He was the 3rd of his mother's children. One of his older brothers had wife who was a Christian. I use to go to church as a child but it had been many years since I been to Church. She was the only one in the party who wasn't drinking or cursing. I remember thinking who do she think she is. Of course I didn't understand or even have a clue what it meant to be a Christian. But Praise God I would later find out. I had a good time with his family and looked forward to being a part of them. I felt love around them and I longed for that from my own family. When we were leaving his sister-in-law told me I could come over anytime. They always had cookouts so I should come over. Well summer was ending and school was coming back. I had to prepare to go back to school which I was not looking forward to. When school ended in June I didn't have a big belly now here it is September and I was showing so I knew my school friends would be surprised. I was now in the 11th grade and I was due to give birth in October. I was tired a lot. My belly was heavy and I just didn't feel like going to school. I figured I would try and stick it out being that I would be out in October to have my baby. When school started I did go back for about a month but by the end of September I was huge and didn't feel like traveling anymore. I decided I would just stay out of school until after I had the baby. My baby father was coming to Brooklyn more often now because it was close to my due date. My mom was allowing him to sleep over but we couldn't sleep together. I did not have my own room so he slept in the basement with my brothers and cousin. My stepfather converted the basement to an apartment so all the guys moved down there. They had it hooked up real fly. That was the hangout spot. My due date had approached and the doctor had me coming to the clinic every week. I was not dilating and they wanted to induce my labor but because I was so young they didn't want to put me through that stress. The doctor decided to wait another week to see if I would go into labor. I was getting stressed and anxious because I was ready to get this baby out of me.

Chapter 17

Someone of My Own to Love

On October 24th they decided to give me a C-Section. I was nervous but kind of happy I was going to get this over with. My baby father was at the hospital with me which helped my fear but I was the one on the operating table. I remember they told me to count from 100 by time I said 100 99 I woke up in so much pain. My stomach felt like a truck had rolled over it. I remember seeing double vision and bright lights all around me. I heard someone calling my name. The nurse was saying to me you had a boy. I remember smiling and being happy that I was alive and I had my baby. They rolled me into the recovery room and I went back to sleep. When I woke up I asked for my baby. The nurse told me he was in the incubator under light because he had Yellow Jaundice. Of course I had no idea what they were talking about but I knew I could not hold him right at that moment. They rolled him to see me and I saw the cutest high yellow curly head fat cheeked baby ever. I instantly fell in love with my son. He looked just like me with his chubby cheeks. I finally had something that belonged to me, something no one could take away from me, something of my own, my son. We hadn't decided on a name during my pregnancy so we were trying to pick out a name. His father wanted him to be named after him being that this was his first child and a son. I didn't like his name to tell you the truth. His biological name was Johnny. I agreed just to please his father. I gave him his father first and last name but I added my own middle name. My son's father didn't have a middle name which was weird to me. I always figured everybody had a middle name. We all had middle names in my family. I was so happy to have my son I didn't care what we named him. His father looked so happy and proud that he had a son. He was showing off our son to everyone that came to my room. My mom worked at Methodist Hospital at the time so a lot of her co-workers came up to see me. You would have thought he was the one who gave birth. Like he did something, I could not even sit up cough or sneeze. I had staples across my stomach in a bikini cut and boy was it painful. I couldn't breast feed because I never fully stopped smoking weed, I just cut down. I had weed in my system when my son was born. Thank God I really don't think they checked back then to see if there were drugs in the babies system. My son was born in 1984. I was in the hospital for 7 days. When I was discharged from the hospital I arrived home to a beautiful reception by my family and friends. There was a sign hanging on my front door telling everyone I had the baby and it was a boy. I didn't have a baby shower which I was kind of disappointed about but it was ok because my baby father brought him all he needed. Motherhood wasn't as easy as I thought it would be. I couldn't take the waking up in the middle of the night or the constant crying. I must say thank God for my mom, she stepped in and took over for me. I didn't know the first thing about being a mother or taking care of a baby. I mean I did help raise my first niece but she didn't belong to me so it was different. I could love her and do her hair which I loved to do but at the end of the day I gave her back to her parents which were my brother and his girlfriend. I had to basically learn how to be a mother, Hold him, feed him, change his diaper, wipe him and burp him. Then I learned what each time he cried meant. The hunger cry, the wet cry, the want to be held cry, the gripe cry and the want attention cry. Parenting was harder than I ever thought it would be. My mom was a great help she would come get him when he was crying and I was getting frustrated. My sister was losing plenty of sleep being that we shared a room. My so would wake up several times in the middle of the night for a bottle. My mom decided to let me to move into the basement. My brother became the super of the building around the corner so his job came with a free apartment. Luckily, they had already converted the basement into an apartment. My boyfriend was spending a lot of time in Brooklyn helping me out with the baby but he would leave and go back to the Bronx at night. He was very helpful and provided my baby with diapers and milk. I couldn't get WIC because my mom worked and I was still a minor under her care so we had to buy everything we needed for the baby. By the beginning of January my baby father decided he wanted to be around my son more often so I asked my mom could he stay with me in the basement. She agreed that he could move in with me but he had to pay rent which was ok with him. By summer time things were going good between us. We were living together and I had decided to go back and finish high school in September. I was back on the hanging out scene. There was a young lady on my block that I became real cool with. I always knew her but we just started hanging out together. We would hang out at each other's house. We smoked week and drank beer together. We started going to the reggae clubs which had begun to pop up all over Brooklyn and queens. I considered her to be one of my best friends. We would talk about everything. She was the only daughter her mom had. She had a brother but he was younger than her. Because she did not have any sisters we became very tight. There wasn't anything I would not do for her or she would not do for me. She use to boost (shoplift) clothes and cosmetics from stores. I wasn't into that type of stuff. I was never a thief or into stealing. I had enough experiences with being in handcuffs so I stayed away from crime. She would boost from expensive stores and she dressed her butt off. I noticed some things that I did not like between her and my boyfriend but I tried not to pay them any attention. She would come to the basement when I was not there. I would be upstairs in my mom house and I came downstairs and she would be sitting in my house with him. I would be like why didn't you come upstairs and she always had an excuse like oh I just decided to wait for you to come down or I just got here. He would be sitting there looking suspicious but again I didn't stress it. I loved and trusted her as a true sister to me. I would go to her house sometimes and she would not answer her door but I could hear her in the apartment. My son father would disappear for hours and I would beep him and he would not answer. I started feeling like something was going on between them. Whenever I couldn't find him she was no were to be found, which was totally not like her. One day a good friend that lived in my building came and told me she saw my son father coming out of my friends building. She said he looked like he was creeping out of the building and did not want to be seen. I said ok I am going to keep my eyes open and watch. Again a few weeks passed and my friend who lived in my building came and said he just went in her building. I ran and I mean ran down the block to her house and started calling up to her window. This was something we always did because her bedroom window was the fire escape. It also was the front so she could hear everything that went on outside including me calling her out of the window. Plus, she lived on the second floor. We would always call her out the window so I knew she heard me. She would not answer me but I had a feeling she was up there. I went upstairs and started banging on her door, still no answer. I was yelling cursing and telling her I know you in there why won't you open the door. I must have banged on the door for about 30 minutes but she would not answer the door for nothing. I knew she was in there and I believed he was there with her. I left after everybody told me to just wait until I see her outside. I was hurt because I never thought she would do something like this to me. Hours later he came home and when he walked in the door I just started swinging on him. I accused him of sleeping with her and I told him when I see her I was going to beat the crap out of her. He was never a good liar so he just stood there trying to deny it but I knew what I was feeling was true. She showed me how guilty she was because I did not see her for a week if not longer. She would avoid coming down the block, instead she would walk all the way around the block. Why avoid me if you are not guilty of something. I felt if she had nothing to hide why was she acting so suspicious. Why didn't she confront me about banging on her door. I know everybody and their momma told her I was out there banging on her door. One day I was on Washington Avenue with my brother and look who I run into, her and her brother walking down the street. I walked up to her and just started swinging on her. We started fighting and I was pulling her by her hair beating the crap out of her. Her brother tried to break it up and my brother grabbed him and started fighting with him. It was a mess but I was so angry that I could have killed her with my bare hands that day. After the fight I told her she better not let me catch her that I was going to fight her every time I saw her. What was so strange was she never asked me what was wrong or why was I fighting her. That was the end of our friendship. Then, because I was miss popularity on the block and everybody liked me people started picking fights with her nobody like her anymore. People started saying she was as a snake and could not be trusted. I think her mom sent her away because I didn't see her for a while after that. As for him, I told him he had to go I didn't want him in my house anymore. This was the second time he cheated on me and I was fed up. This was worse because he did this on my block. I mean was he serious we had a child together. How could he do this to me? My mom actually took his side and said he don't have to leave. I was furious with my mother for not standing up for me. I knew it was because he was paying her rent but I figured my happiness should come first. Then again I thought about it, my mom never had my back in most situations anyway so I wasn't surprised. I decided I was going to pay him back and start cheating on him as well. I decided I wasn't going back to High School since they wanted to put me back in the 11th grade. They had every right to because I dropped out at the beginning of the school year. I decided I would go to a Vocational School which Eramus Hall helped me apply for. I got accepted to SCS Business and Technical Institute Down town Brooklyn on Willoughby Street. This program also went by another mane called Helen Keller School for the Blind. I was in a school with handicapped and disabled people and I began to appreciate my life and realize how blessed I truly was. I didn't really know what a blessing was but I did know I felt sorry for the students in my school. They were blind, handicapped and some were in wheelchairs. I didn't stay there long because I had a small child at home. My mom use to work nights but when she did overtime during the day she could not watch my son. I missed a lot of days in school. I started messing with a guy in my building who I always liked but my baby daddy was there so that couldn't work out. Well since I was angry and paying him back I decided to start seeing the guy. I would sneak into him house when his mother was at work and we would have sex. He had a girlfriend but I didn't care, for me it was just sex no strings attached. One day she popped up over his house and I was there and she hit the ceiling. I don't know if she thought I would be scared of her but I was ready to fight her. She was older than I was so she looked at me as a kid. She started coming over his house everyday just to make sure I wasn't there. Little did she know I was there during the day while she was at work. We use to smoke weed together and have sex. We feel in love with each other but his girlfriend and my baby daddy was in the way. One day she went to my mother and asked her to tell me to leave him alone. That was a joke my mom couldn't tell me who to screw. My mother told her she couldn't do anything with me I was grown. Which I really wasn't but I sure acted grown. She would walk pass me and make faces and say smart things to me but she never stepped to me. I think it was because she knew I would be ready to fight her. I'm sure she didn't want anyone to think she was fighting over no man. Personally, I really didn't care I was young and didn't care. There was a fire in his apartment and they had to jump out of the window. Thank God they lived on the first floor and no one was hurt. I remember feeling like thank goodness it wasn't me in his house when the fire happened. The apartment wasn't badly damaged but they had to leave for a while until the apartment was habitable again. He would still come hang out on the block so I still got to see him. I loved his mom also she cook the best West Indian food ever. They were from Barbados but you wouldn't know it because he was more Americanized. I wasn't to use to West Indian food, they use too many spices for me but her food was good. I was glad when they finished doing the renovations on his apartment he came back and I was back in his bed.

Chapter 18

The Crack Era – a Nightmare

So, now let me introduce you to the crack era. It came in like a vengeance and boy did it hit hard. Everybody and they momma was getting high on crack. They would either lace the weed with it or smoke it in a cigarettes. The more addicted addicts would free base which was a direct high because they smoked it in a crack pipe. When it first hit the streets I didn't want any parts of it. I didn't see what the big deal was. Well I would soon find out. Women were selling their bodies for this drug. Men were robbing their own mommas and their own homes for this drug. People were being killing over this drug. The drug business was booming big time from this epidemic. So many people I knew were on crack but at the time I was still fixed on my weed. Being a new mom I didn't have time to get addicted to any hard drugs. Or so I thought. By now my son father was going back and forth to court for this drug case. He had already told me he was most likely going to do some jail time. He decided to cope out which is plead guilty to the charge so you could do less time. Especially if you were guilty and they had a good case against you as was the case with him. He was caught in the drug spot with the evidence. He ended up getting sentenced to 1 to 3 years for his old drug arrest in the Bronx. They gave him a date to start his sentence which he had to turn himself in. I was sad because he was a good father to my son. He was very supportive in every way though we were no longer together he didn't neglect his father responsibilities. He was there for my son and that was fine with me. I was doing me. He wanted to get back together with me but I wasn't having it. He had broken my heart one time to many and this time I was done. I remember the day he had to turn himself in to jail. He had to go to the courthouse downtown Brooklyn and from there they would remand him to jail. I cried when he left because I knew I wouldn't see him for a while. Once he got to Rikers Island jail in Queens he called me. They are allowed a collect call so my mom said it was ok for him to call us collect. I went to the jail a few days later to see him. I hated seeing him in that orange jumpsuit. I felt sorry for him. The visit was only an hour and I figured it took me almost three hours to get there just to spend an hour. They were sending him upstate and he asked me to come see him when he got upstate. I couldn't say no after all he took care of me and was always in my corner. Once he went upstate I did go and see him. I liked that jail better because the visit was eight hours long and we were able to walk around and eat food and snacks out of the vending machine. We also was able to talk pictures. He wanted me to bring our son up there but I told him no plus my mom wasn't having that at all. I didn't want my son up there either. Though he was only months old I didn't want him exposed to the elements of jail. A new game room opened up on Washington Avenue which became a spot to hangout. There were games and a pool table but that was a front for the weed that they sold in the back of the store. My brother started selling weed in the game room with this guy we will call Paul who I never seen before. I would go there just to see the guy. He was cute, dark skin with a heavy West Indian accent. I told my brother I liked his friend and my brother was like don't mess with him. I wanted to know why. My brothers was always overprotective of me so I just figured he didn't want me messing with his friends. Well I would go to the game room when my brother wasn't there and flirt with his friend. Eventually, I started messing with my brother friend Paul. The game room became the place to be. You could buy your weed, hang out in the back and smoke it. I loved the game room and I liked the guy that was working in there. I really didn't know much about him but I planned on getting to know him better. I would go into the game and act like I was looking for my brother. I could tell Paul liked me as well. He seemed real quiet with me like he didn't want to say much to me. I think he did not want to mess with me because I was his friends little sister. He always had a serious look on his face like he didn't smile a lot. I figured because was new to the neighborhood and he sold weed he stayed himself. One day I was in the game room and Paul asked me how old I was.

He knew I had a son but he didn't know my age. I was very sassy at that time so I answered old enough. I think he liked me because I seemed like a challenge. We started messing around on the down low so no one knew. I would go to the game room and hang out in the back room with him. No one knew I was back there because you couldn't see from the front. There was a room back there with a bathroom, a bed, T.V. and a stash for the weed and money. I would lay in the bed smoking weed while he was in front handling the customers. A lot of kids came in to play games so he had quarters for the games. When my brother found out I was messing with Paul he wasn't too happy about it, but I was grown and he couldn't do anything about it. So back to the crack epidemic. Crack was the drug of choice by now that was where the money was. No one was smoking weed anymore. My new boyfriend Paul was now selling crack which was much more profitable, it was more expensive then weed. More and more people were doing crack. I personally knew a whole bunch of people who were using it and dealing it. Paul had his own place. He was renting a kitchenette on Halsey Street. I loved it because it was comfortable and cozy. He had a large room, his own kitchen and a very tiny bathroom. I would go to his house and hang out with him after he closed the game room. My mom would watch my son I had to put him to sleep before I left the house. I looked forward to going to his house, it became like a nightly thing. When I first had sex with him I really enjoyed it. He would treat me so good body massages, feet rubs. I never had a man who caressed my body like he did. We were having plenty of sex. He was from Barbados and he didn't have any kids. I like him because he seemed like he was all into me. He had a car which I loved. He was the first I had a man who owned his own vehicle. I enjoyed riding around sitting in the front seat with him, I felt like I was hot stuff because my man had a car. We would go buy food, go to his house, smoke weed and make love. I was no longer having sex I was making love that's how good he made me feel. We had been dating for about 5 months and he decided he wanted to stop working in the game room and go into business for himself. Which he told me he had planned on going to business for his self after he saved up enough money. He knew the connections since he was already I in the drug game. I had family members who were in the drug game so I knew how much the business could profit. He was tired of working for other people and wanted to make his own money. He was tired of selling drugs for other people when he could make his own money. I was all for it because I loved money. Paul brought some cocaine and tried selling it. He figured he would start there, but no one was doing cocaine anymore. Cocaine was considered the white man drug because it was so expensive and black people really couldn't afford it. I didn't like cocaine. People either sniffed cocaine or lace it in your cigarettes or weed. I tried it before but I didn't like the high it gave me. I put it in a cigarette and it made my heart race. It even tried sniffing it but that didn't work out for me. I always suffered with bad allergies so I had a problem with sniffing something up my nose. I didn't want anything in my nose but tissue. One time when I tried to sniff coke, I ended up blowing the coke off of the straw. Everybody who I was getting high with got mad at me. That was it for me I didn't try that anymore. There was another time I tried a drug that wasn't for me. That drug was P-FUNK. I remember my Paul and some family members were smoking it, I decided I wanted to try it. They had it rolled up in bamboo paper so it looked like a joint. They kept telling me I didn't need to try it but me and my hardheaded tail insisted on trying it. I took two puffs off the joint and that was the last thing I remember. I immediately got dizzy and felt light headed. I didn't even realize I had passed out. When I came to I was fully dressed standing in the shower, they were holding me up so I wouldn't fall down. They put me in my bed and let me sleep it off before my mom came home from work. I will never forget how it made me feel and I never ever tried that drug again. I was sick as a dog the next day I had diarrhea and nausea. Thank God he took that desire for that drug away from me quick fast. Again, I did not know how much God was covering my life then, but glory be to God I would soon find out. Paul was now buying cocaine and cooking it up to turn it into crack cocaine. He taught me how to cook it and turn the cocaine into an 8 ball which was what it was called back then. Cooking it was very easy and I became a regular chemist. Not boasting or bragging but I'm being truthful. But wait it gets worse. I started helping him cook, cut it up and cap the crack to sell. We had twenties and dimes which were selling like hotcakes. We sold the crack from capsules. They were different sizes and colors according to the value of the crack. First let me say I take no pleasure in writing this, but if I am going to tell the story I want to tell the truth. At one point business was so good that he was able to hire a worker to help him sell the drugs. I wasn't involved in the selling of the drugs but I did help him process it. I remember wondering what the big deal about this crack. Business was so good that Paul was selling out every day. He went from cooking one eight ball to two and three a day. Business was booming and I was loving it. We had so much money coming in that it was unreal. Thousands of dollars a week. The sad reality of this was I didn't see the destruction it was causing to lives and families. I still repent of my sins to this very day. I didn't understand that hurting someone for my own gain was not what my heavenly father created me for. I can truly say I'm sorry for my past but it helped to shape and create my future my testimony. When I tell you that God is so good it is because I am a living testimony to his goodness. After a while the guy who was selling the crack for us started using it. We had to fire him because he could no longer be trusted. I tell you this crack was something else. He went through worker after worker and they all would succumb to the same result getting addicted to the drugs. One day Paul decided we would try our own drugs. Let me explain. When you cook up the cocaine you add baking soda which gives it the solid substance called crack. . If too much baking soda is used you could lose the potency of the drug so you had to always make sure you had the right measurement. So what he decided was instead of having testers which were people who would test your product we would test it ourselves. Now I was not using any crack whatsoever neither did I have a desire to use it. I was so blinded by love that when he suggested I test it I wasn't thinking about the potential for addiction it had. I was in love so of course I am going to do what it takes to please my man. After all he was taking care of me and my son. I really didn't think I would be doing this drug on a regular I was supposed to just try it out. I remember the first time I used crack it was immediately addictive. I liked the way it made me feel. I liked the rush it gave me. It had a sweet taste to it so it was something you could enjoy. I remember wanting more and more after the first time I tried it.

Chapter 19

Addiction

Business was booming. People were pawning their jewelry, TV's, Brand new clothes, Sneakers and everything they could get their hands on. On some occasions I heard mothers were trying to use their children as collateral for payment of drugs. I had so much jewelry from drug addicts selling their valuables and honestly I loved it. I use to think how stupid they were for pawning their possessions for drugs. I didn't know the extent of this addiction until it hit me as hard. Paul was dealing so much drugs that we had money just to waste. He use to give me fifteen dollars a day just for spending money plus he was still selling weed so I had access to all the weed I wanted. Now this was the late 80's so $15 dollars a day was a lot of money to have in your pocket. That's when the dollar still had value. As time went on I noticed Paul was changing. He began to become very aggressive towards me always wanting to argue. I thought it was because the drug business was stressful so I excused his behavior. I didn't know at the time that I was dating a ticking time bomb waiting to explode and boy oh boy did he explode. Thank you Jesus I am alive today to tell my testimony. But by the grace of God. I watched his behavior spiral out of control. He would go from being a calm loving caring individual to a ball of fire ranting and raving and cursing. I remember the first time Paul hit me like it was yesterday. It is amazing how memories stay in your head especially memories that had such a profound impact on your life. I had never been through domestic violence. I was always the aggressor in any situation when it came to violence. I wasn't use to any man beating me. My son's father was on no way violent. Now, I had endured a lot in my young life but nothing prepared me for what I was about to go through. If I don't know anything else, I know for sure it was truly the Grace and Mercy of God that got me through the many obstacles in my life. I took my son and went to spend the day over Paul house. I don't normally take my son over his house because of the nature of his business. Though he didn't sell drugs out of his house he had all the paraphernalia there which he used on a daily basis. This day he was arguing with me as always over whatever he felt like picking an argument about. I was holding my son on my lap sitting at the table next to the window. There was a small radiator under the window and I would sometimes lean on it to look out the window. For some reason I was a little afraid of his behavior this particular argument. He kept getting in my face acting like he was going to hit me. I put my son on my lap to try and defuse his anger. I figured my son being there would curb some of his ranting. Well I was wrong. Before I knew he slapped me in my face so hard that I fell out of the chair and my head hit the radiator. I woke up yes woke up laying across the bed. First thing I thought about when I came to was what just happened and where's my son? Once I was able to focus because I had a splitting headache, I saw my son sitting on the bed next to me. My man was coming from the bathroom with a cloth in his hand. I realize the cloth was for the huge knot on my forehead which happened when I hit my head on the radiator. I couldn't even move my body I was in so much pain especially my head. My son was looking at me like what happened to you but he wasn't crying. I could tell he had been crying but he must have stopped. I needed to get to the bathroom so I could look at my head. I felt the knot but I needed to see what it looked like. I could not believe this man just hit me and with such force it knocked me out of the chair. Furthermore, my son was on my lap and he didn't even care about that. I tried to get up off the bed and he came to help me up. I told him to leave me alone. I could not believe this dude just hit me. I asked him why you do this to me why did you hit me. He started telling me how sorry, but in the same breath he started blaming me talking about I made him hit me. Really!! One minute we arguing the next minute I woke up on the bed not even remembering what happened to me. When I got in the bathroom I looked in the mirror and there was a big round swollen knot sitting on my forehead. I didn't know how I was going to go home with this knot on my head. It wasn't like I could hide it. I started crying telling him look what you did to me my face is ruined. He came in the bathroom and started hugging me acting like he was sorry for what he did. I knew I could not let my brothers or cousin see my face because they would want to fight him. One thing about my family we may have had our differences like any other family has but let some beef go down and it will be on. I remember my cousin had some problems where she lived in Atlantic Terminals and she called us. I gathered my crew and we went down there to do damage. I knew this was not going to sit well with them. I decided to stay at his house until the swelling went down. I called my mom and she wanted my son home, she acted like he belonged to her. I lied and told her I was coming home the next day knowing I would be at his house for at least a week. We were putting stuff on my head to take the swelling down. About 3 days later the swelling finally went down and I went home. My face was still bruised but it didn't look as bad as when it first happened. I lied and told everybody I walked into the door. I knew no one believed me. After a few days passed I went back to his house because he kept begging me to come over. He promised he would never hit me again. I wanted to believe him so I gave him a second chance. By now we are using the drugs heavily ourselves. It started out as testing the potency of it, then occasionally using to getting high to smoking crack just about every day. We were using more than he was selling. We would mix it with weed or cigarettes called 'Lacing' or "Woolers". Most people smoked the crack pipe but I was too cute to see myself smoking off somebodies crack pipe. I thought we could stop using at any time because weed was my main drug of choice. Every time I was at my man house we ended up getting high and having sex. Actually I think the sex got better when we were high or though it seemed. See that's what drug addiction does to you it distorts your thinking. He decided he wanted to move to another place. A lot of his dealer friends knew where we lived so he wanted more privacy. He found a better kitchenette in a better area of Brooklyn. I liked this place better plus it was bigger than the other place. We had much more space. The good thing about moving was dealers and users didn't know where we were living so they couldn't come begging for credit. I enjoyed this lifestyle I was living. Selling drugs, using drugs, having all the drugs I wanted seemed like the perfect life for me. But, Life will teach you lessons real fast. My man started getting verbally abusive with me calling me out of my name. The name calling got so bad that I forget my name was Vanessa. He would argue about any and everything. I guess he figured since he was taking care of me and supplying me with drugs, he had a right to treat me as he pleased. One time when Paul was verbally abusing me I decided to stand up for myself and argue back. He was yelling at me and got in my face so I pushed him to get him out of my face. Before I could fully get to push him, he head butted me in my forehead. Now I never in my life been head butt, truthfully I didn't even know what it was called until it happened to me. One minute we are arguing and the next minute I'm on the floor. What's crazy is he didn't physically hit me with his hands. He took his forehead and banged it on top of my forehead with enough force to knock me to the floor. I was dumbfounded and confused. I'm here thinking did this man just hit me with his head. I mean what do you think when someone hit you with their forehead. He was standing over me looking at me like get up and I will head butt you again. I now knew I was dealing with a fool. I had never been through no mess like this and I had been through a lot. I never been through no man beating me so I didn't know what to do. The sad part was I loved him so how do I handle this. I get my family to beat the crap out of him or do I keep believing him when he say it won't happen again.

Chapter 20

My Nightmare with Domestic Violence

Well I stayed with him thinking he was really sorry and it would never happen again. How wrong I was. He went from slapping me to head butting me, to punching me with closed fist. I remember having to watch what I said which was hard for me because I was always a sassy mouth child. It got so bad that any little thing would set him off. If I sucked my teeth he would slap me. If I rolled my eyes he would slap me. If I talked back to him he would slap me. Eventually, I became afraid of him. I literally felt like I had to walk on egg shells around him. I thought maybe the drugs was making him act like this. I was just making excuses for him. He always had this behavior in him I would soon find out. I'm sure I wasn't the first female he beat. I later found out I would not be the last. Paul ended up doing 10 years in jail after he got deported for almost killing his girlfriend in Barbados, but well get to that later. The beating would only get worse. Black eyes, busted lips, numerous bruises, kicking me with boots on, to say the least. His favorite was dragging me by my hair. We were walking down Fulton Street in Brooklyn one day and he was yelling at me because he thought I made eye contact with some guy. He grabbed me and starts slapping me right there in the street. People were looking and he started asking them what the blank they were looking at. I was more embarrassed then ashamed. If he even thought I was looking at another guy he would beat me when we got to his house. He would act all sweet while we were outside but the moment we got behind closed doors he would jump on me. I didn't even like going out in the street with him because he would always find a reason to argue when we got back to his house. I know the 10,000 question is why stay in an abusive relationship? Why didn't I leave him or get him locked up. FEAR. Fear that he would kill me as he had threatened to do many times before and when you have someone who pulls a gun on you, you tend to believe that they could hurt you. He would beat me until blood was coming out of my nose. It seemed like he had to see blood before he would stopped. My family members and friends noticed I was acting different. My behavior was different I became withdrawn. I wasn't as happy and outgoing as I use to be. None of my friends like him. I had gay friends that I loved so much. They have since passed away but they will always be dear to my heart. They were the best friends you would ever want to have. They were Loving, caring, kind and would give you the shirt off their back. Paul hated them. He was so anti-gay. He had a gay phobia like he was not sure about his own sexuality. I mean why else would you hate people just because of their sexual preference. I am not God so I have no right to judge anyone and my past hasn't always been squeaky clean either. I have been far from perfect. Whenever my friends came around and he was around he would make me leave with him. They witnessed him pulling my hair and dragging me several times. They didn't like him either but because I loved him they stayed out of it. No one knew I was smoking crack with him, I was too ashamed to tell anyone. That wasn't a conversation you had with people unless they were getting high as well. To my surprise I found out just about the whole block I lived on was smoking woolies that was the name for smoking laced crack. I still didn't want my business out there though. I also realized some people close to me were using as well. This drug was tearing families and homes apart. The beatings from my man were getting worse. He loved pulling his gun out and pointed it at me. I was petrified. He always threaten to kill me if I cheated on him. I was too scared to cheat on this fool. He had me shook. I watched him go from a sweet giving kind person to a monster in a matter of a year. I should have ran when I had the chance but I loved him and wanted to make it work. Plus, I enjoyed the drugs he was giving me. Sad but true. We moved once again and I say we because I was at his house more then I was at my own house. I notice I was feeling nauseous in the mornings. I felt I was pregnant but wasn't sure. I remember how I felt when I was pregnant with my son and it was similar to what I began to feel. One morning I woke up and started throwing up. I told him I thought I might be pregnant.

He immediately went and brought me a pregnancy test. Wouldn't you know it I was pregnant. He literally stood over me as I took the text so he knew before I even said anything. He was so happy. This was his first kid. Paul told me you are keeping the baby. He didn't ask me what I wanted to do or even gave me an option. He basically made the decision for me. Personally, I had mixed feelings because I knew I would never be able to get rid of him. He was verbally, mentally and physically abusive, on top of being very controlling, why would I want to have a baby with this nut. I don't know it that's a question or a statement. I knew I would be doing more harm than good to myself by having his child but I was too afraid tom have an abortion. If he didn't know it would be different but he knew so I couldn't sneak behind his back.

.

Chapter 21

Meeting His Family

He told me he wanted me to meet his mom. I wasn't sure I wanted him telling everyone o was pregnant because I truly didn't wasn't to be with him anymore. I was afraid of him and I knew having a child with him was only going to give him a reason to think he owned me. I decided I would go with him to meet his mom I really didn't have a choice. I was too afraid to have an abortion. I probably would have had to go into hiding had I killed his child. Finally one day he brought me a new outfit and got my hair done for me which at this time I use to wear my hair braided a lot. Adding extensions to your hair was the new fade and I was so lucky they had extensions that were the exact color of my hair. My hair have no name for the color but a number, isn't that funny. God have a since of humor. As I said before I hated the color of my hair and I wanted black hair so bad. I hated being different. I even went as far as to have one of my best friends who we are still friends to this day and I'm talking over 30 years braid my hair in black extension hair. It looked awful and I mean awful. I took it out in two days. He took me to meet him family which I must say I loved them. His mom came straight from heaven. She had a big beautiful smile and treated me like she knew me forever. The first day she met me she fed me and I am talking about a huge plate of food. I don't know if I looked hungry but she surely fed me. The food was delicious. Now I know where he got his cooking skills from. He has two sisters who are twins. They are fraternal twins one is tall, one is short, one is slim, one is thick, if you didn't know they were twins you would not know because they don't look identical. Thought they did dress alike when I first met them. His sisters were so sweet and innocent you could tell they were still pure unlike me. I already had a child, and had been through all kinds of trail and tribulations. I've been Molested, tried to commit suicide, ran away from home, stabbed someone, arrested twice, used drugs, sold drugs, and now domestic violence victim and I was only 19 years old. He told his family I was pregnant and they were happy. They all were hugging me and asking me a thousand questions. How many months was I? When was the baby coming? I wasn't even showing yet. He is his mom's oldest child and her only son so this baby was special to them. She had no grandchildren so I knew my baby would be extra spoiled. Even though he was abusive I thought maybe the baby would change him. My thinking was what do I have to lose? I'm already his girlfriend and he takes care of me and my son. Even though he is abusive maybe it will get better now that I was pregnant. I didn't think he would be hitting me anymore. I was so WRONG. Things went downhill at lightning speed. I had made an appointment to see the doctor at Methodist Hospital where my son was born. As I waited for the appointment he became over bearing. I loved Red Devil hot sauce and I love to put it all over my food. Well, he decided he didn't want me eating hot sauce anymore because it would hurt the baby so I couldn't eat hot sauce which I loved. Especially on some fried chicken. I would put it on everything. He stopped me from smoking cigarettes which wasn't a bad thing. His attitude and controlling behavior just got worse because now he felt like now he owned me, like I was property or cattle. The beatings didn't stop either. Whenever he wanted to start a fight with me he would. If the kool-aid wasn't sweet enough that called for a slap. If it was too sweet he would hit me. If I over cooked the white rice which I did on a regular because I never could properly cook rice, I either overcooked it or it was too hard. He would beat me. He would drag me by my hair over rice. I always had bruises being so light well he had a remedy for that, He started kicking me. He had a way of pulling his foot bad and kicking me like he was kicking a soccer ball. It hurt a lot because he did it with such force. He would kick me in my leg or lower back so the bruise wouldn't show. His favorite was head butting. During his tyrants I watch his hands to be on guard to block my face when he swung at me, but he would head butt me which always caught me by surprise. Thank God I don't have brain damage from all the head trauma he inflicted on me. I knew I had to tell my mom I was pregnant I just wasn't ready.

I knew she would not be happy at all. Mind you I still had Fino my son father in jail and though we weren't together I think he really thought when he came out of jail there was a possibility of him and I getting back together. I really didn't want to get back together with him but I did miss him. I finally got up the courage to tell my mom about being pregnant. I really didn't care if she was upset because I was older and I could make my own decisions, plus I really wasn't living in her house anymore. I still had a bed and clothes there but physically I stayed out almost every night. He would give my mother money for watching my son when I wasn't there, besides most of the time my son was sleep when I left the house for the night. My sister moved into her own apartment in Flatbush. I finally had my own room for the first time in my life. I was glad to finally have my own room. That was short lived because but my mom put my niece in the room with me. I didn't care because she was still little but I still needed my space. I was tired of not having my own. When I told my mom about me being pregnant was not happy at all. She felt I was irresponsible with my son so what did I possible need with another child. She was right in a since because I was his mother but she was his caretaker. Honestly I didn't need another child but I wanted my baby. Again, it felt good having something of my own. Though my mom wasn't too happy, his mom was ecstatic. After all this was her first grandchild. My mom already had 4 grandchildren by this time. We started going to his mom house on a regular basis. He had friends over there that were in the drug game as well I loved going over there because she would cook a feast. I fell in love with her West Indian cooking. My mom could cook her butt off but this was a different culture so the food was different. My mom cooked southern style and she cook Caribbean style so it was the best of both worlds. At first he was being so good to me. I went to the doctor and confirmed my pregnancy. He was right along with me supporting me every step of the way. The beatings stopped for a while, I guess because he didn't want to hurt our baby. I stopped getting high because I wanted a healthy baby. I also had a friend who had a baby that was born premature due to her drug addiction. When I went with her to the hospital to see her baby I remember I cried because her baby was so small she fit in the palm of her hand. Praise God today my friend daughter is healthy and she have her own child. My determination to stop using drugs was short lived. I started getting high again while I was pregnant. I guess in part because he had it around me. It was hard to kick the addiction with the drugs right in my face. He would give me the crack to smoke, then beat me for getting high. This was insane. The beatings weren't as brutal as before but I still had to walk on egg shells around him. I had to watch what I said or he would slap me in my mouth. I couldn't sucked my teeth at him he would hit me. He hit me for just about any and everything. I went back to my mom house as my pregnancy grew. I knew I would need my mom help with the baby. He wasn't happy with me being back at my mom house, he couldn't beat or control me over there. My family was there so I felt safe and protected. One time my mom was at work no one was in the house with us and he wanted to have sex. One thing I didn't do is have sex in my mom house. First of all we never locked our apartment door. We had a large family living there so there was always in and out traffic. My Step-father was the super so he was always in and out of the house. I was afraid we would be having sex in the house and someone would walk in and catch us. I didn't have a lock on my bedroom door so there was no real privacy. He started choking me because I didn't want to have sex. I could not breath that's how hard he was choking me. My stepfather came in the house and my daughter father took his hands from around my neck. The only reason he stopped choking me was because my step pops came in. He knocked on my door which was closed and looked in the room. I was grasping for air. My stepfather asked me what was wrong and I lied and said I wasn't feeling good but I believe he knew it was more to it than that. I was about seven months pregnant so I stayed close to home. Him and I would go to his mom house and hang out with his sisters. I liked being around them. I preferred to be out with him then to be in his house. He was less likely to fight me in the street. When he got angry there was no controlling him, I didn't want to chance him beating me and hurting the baby. We went shopping for baby clothes and I was so excited. He didn't want anyone feeling like they had to take care of my baby. He had a lot of pride. Plus, this was his first child so he wanted to do everything that needed to be done. I still had the bassinette and crib from my son. I hardly used them because he slept in my bed with me most of the time. After we left his mom house, I ended up going back to his house with him. That night I told him I am going to stay at my mom house after the baby was born because I would probably have another C-section and I would need my mom to help me. He wasn't very happy about this but he agreed. When we got to his house he started preparing the crack for sale for the next day. One thing about him he didn't trust anyone so he had a cut off time as to when he would be in the streets selling crack. I was back to cooking and helping him prepare the drugs. So I was back to getting high again. The temptation to use was to strong and fight off. I mean it was right in my face, under my nose, my hands was touching it and it drew me right back in. I here I am getting high again and it hit my eighth month pregnant. He was allowing me to get high actually he was getting high with me. He started using crack a couple of months after me and of course he blamed me for him getting high. I couldn't understand why he would beat me for getting high but he would give the drugs to me. I guess it was because he wanted to keep me dependent and submissive to him. He knew he had the drugs and I wanted them so he used them to keep me at my lowest. Basically, he was my drug supplier. He knew as long as he piled me up with drugs that I would stay at his house. We would get high as a kite and have sex all night. He made sure he went with me to every doctor appointment. That was just another way of wanting to be in control of every move I made. At the appointment the doctor said my baby had a slow heart beat which was detected by the Sonogram. The doctor wanted to know was I taking any medication other than my vitamins and iron pills. Of course I didn't want to tell them I was smoking crack so I lied and said no I was not. I was seven months at this time and I knew this was a critical time for the baby development, but the addiction had a hold on me. I still wanted to get high even though I had a full term baby inside of me. The doctor told me to come back the next day to take a sonogram. Of course I didn't show up because I knew they would find drugs in my system. Since I had an appointment the following week, I decided to wait and go back for my pre-natal checkup. The following week, I went back to the doctor for my pre-natal appointment and they decided to give me a sonogram. During the sonogram they determined my baby had an irregular heartbeat, whatever that meant and they wanted to do an emergency C-section in the morning. I wanted to wait until I went in labor to give birth but they made it seem as though it was a life or death situation for my baby. So I agreed to come back the next morning to be admitted for the C-section which they said they would do first thing in the morning. I was glad because I wanted to get high one last time before I had to stay in the hospital for seven days, which was the amount of time they kept you after a C-section. Well I didn't tell him what the doctor told me. He wasn't in the room with me during my examination so he didn't hear everything. We went to eat and after that we went to his house. That night we got high. I didn't even take into consideration that the doctor told me my baby had an irregular heartbeat. I was just concerned about putting the drugs in my system. The sad part in writing about this now brings back so many regrets because I didn't see the seriousness of the addiction I had. The next morning I went to my mom house to tell her they wanted to do an emergency C-section on me. I should have told her the night before but I didn't want anything to interfere with me getting high. She was pissed because she had to now make arrangements at the last minute for someone to watch my son while she was at work. I have a very good friend who I am still friends with to this very day who ended up helping my mom out by watching my son for her. All that day I noticed my baby wasn't moving much but I did feel some movement just not as much as I had felt before. After getting high one last time, the next day I decided to go to the hospital which is now two days after they originally scheduled me to have the baby.

Chapter 22

Giving Birth to My Daughter

I went to the hospital without any clothes or toiletries that's how high I still was I wasn't thinking clearly. When I got to the hospital and told them I came for a C-section they called my doctor. He told them to admit me and he would perform the surgery in the morning. I had already eaten and you cannot eat before surgery. They did my Vital signs which were my blood pressure and temperature. My blood pressure was high. That evening my baby father came to the hospital with a care bag. It had everything I needed, a Night gown, lotion, deodorant, and some other items. I wished he had brought me a blunt to smoke. The next day they came into the room early in the morning to take me into the operating room. As they were prepping me for surgery I was shaking on the operating table. I didn't feel well, I guess my body was craving the drugs. My doctor asked me was I ok and I told him I had something to tell him. I started crying as admitted to getting high during my pregnancy. I felt it was best to be honest. He asked me when the last time I used drugs. I told him about 2 days ago. Which was a lie because I got high the night before. The doctor decided to lower the dosage of anesthesia they were going to give me because they didn't know how much drugs was in my system. They asked me what kind of drugs I was doing and I admitted to smoking crack laced with marijuana. I felt embarrassed because the doctors and midwives were looking at me like I was dirt. They started whispering to each other like I wasn't even there. Though I was ashamed of myself, I was happy I admitted it. At least

they would know how to treat me and my baby just in case I had any compli-
cations. The medicine they gave me during the surgery was very light because
they had to monitor me considering what I had just told them. I felt the pressure and everything they were doing to me, but I wasn't in pain because I was
still sedated. When I woke after the C-section they had me in the recovery
room. I asked the nurse what did I have and she said a girl. I asked could I see
my baby and she said she was in the baby intensive care unit. I immediately
asked why and she said a social worker was coming to talk to me. I was so nervous. Here I am laying here in pain and they tell me a social worker have to
come speak to me. I already knew it was about my drug use. When the social
worker came to talk to me she told me my baby was born with drugs in her
system. She went on to say she was experiencing drug induced tremors because
her body was craving the drugs. Every time I got high she got high. The drugs
I was using was going into her blood stream. All I could do was lay there and
cry. They had to give her some special cocktail of medications to detox her
and she would be in the hospital until all the drugs were out of her system.
She said, because I lived with my mom they would allow me to take my baby
home but I would be under strict supervision. They also had to open up an
ACS case against me, and since there was another child involved which was
my son, I was going to be under the microscope by the agency. I decided drugs
was not worth me losing my children so I wasn't going to get high anymore.
They let me take my daughter home with the agreement that my mom was
going to be her guardian. I said ok to that they gave my mom a caseworker
and she would be enrolled in the foster kinship program where they would
give her money for taking care of my kids. I knew they would be in good hands
so I didn't mind plus I was living in the house with them. I would have to con-
sent to drug test whenever they wanted me to. I would have to give urine.
After I brought my daughter I was doing good not getting high. About a
month after she was born I got high again with my daughters father. What a
fool I was. I knew they were going to be doing random drug test but I figured
since they had not tested me in a month it wasn't that serious. Well baby was
I wrong. The very next day the ACS worker popped up at my mom house and
asked for some urine. I knew I was doomed. Of course a few days later they
came back and said my drug test came back positive and I could not live in the
house with the kids anymore. I was devastated. I had no one to blame but myself I knew it was my own fault. I had to have supervised visits which meant I

couldn't be left alone with my own kids. I had to go stay with my daughter father which I really didn't want to because he was my supplier, abuser and my enabler. He wanted me to be dependent on him which I already was. Well, now it was even worse because I couldn't go back to live at my mom house. My son father came home from jail and my family welcomed him back with open arms. They always loved my son father he was like family whereas on the other hand they didn't like my daughter father because he was abusive to me. Things got even uglier because daughter father was upset because my son father was always at my mom house. Which was good for my mom because he was able to take my son off her hands for a few hours. I would go to my mom house to see the kids and my daughter father swore I was cheating with Fino which I really wasn't. It had been almost three years since we broke up and I was not even thinking about that man. Every time I went to my mom house when I got home he would beat me up. He just wanted a reason to hit me and that was perfect for him. He was constantly accusing me of cheating on him so he could hit me. And it wasn't just a hit, it was always a close fist punch or a head butt. I was so tired of him hitting on me but I felt like I was trapped. I was in a loveless relationship to afraid to get out. Afraid for my life, afraid for my safety.

Chapter 23

He Isolated Me from My Family

We moved yet again to Herkimer Street between Buffalo and Rochester Avenue. I noticed every time we moved it was always further and further away from my family. Which was perfect for him because he wanted me away from my kids my family and my friends. Totally dependent on him. Of course the beatings started again now I had no one to run to being all the way across town. One day he was beating me and I was screaming so loud that the next door neighbor called the cops. When the cops came they asked me what happened. It was obvious that I was beat up my face was bruised up. I told the officers he hit me but that it was my fault because I made him do it. The cops arrested him. He tried to resist but the cops threw him to the floor and cuffed him. I felt so bad that they were roughing him up. I didn't know what to do this was the first time he got arrested for beating me. I had to go to the court the next day and I lied and said he did not hit me. He got released because I refused to press charges. The judge knew I was lying but there weren't any witnesses to the beating so he had to let him go. The judge gave me and order of protection and told him to stay away from me. That meant nothing to him because I lived in his house. Also, this was the 3rd order of protection I had and I never went back to court to follow up. After leaving court, I wanted to go to my mom house because I knew he was going to beat me again for him getting arrested but I had no place to go. That night he beat my butt again for making him get arrested. He beat me with his leather belt like he was beating his child. I ran and tried to hide under the bed but he flipped over the whole bed mattress and box spring to get to me. He wrapped his fingers in my hair and pound my face like I was a punching bag. He then dragged me by my hair across the floor causing my knees to bleed from the wood on the floor. I have scars to his very day. He kneaded me in the stomach, kicked me, stomp on me, and spit on me. When he finally finished I was laying on the floor like a limp rag doll. Then he went into the bathroom got my wash rag and wash my face, wipe my tears and tell me how sorry he was and why do I make him to this to me that it would never happen again. I was so use to this scenario that it didn't even affect me anymore. I was numb to everything now. I could feel the pain but it was surreal like you know this is happening but it don't seem real. It only got worse. I believe it was because he knew I had no place to go so the torture began. First he would pour any kind of liquid on me from the top of my head. The liquid would run all through my hair on to my clothes. Soda, Juice, Sorrell, Peanut Punch, Water whatever he felt like pouring on me he would. It got worse now the real torture began. He would pull out his gun threaten to use it pointing it in my face. He would make me look down the barrel of the gun with the gun pointed right at my eye ball. I was traumatized. I was afraid that as I was looking down the barrel of the gun he would pull the trigger. My body would shake uncontrollably. He played Russian roulette with me, which once I peed on myself I was so scared. Russian roulette is when you take the gun and put one bullet in the chamber and pull the trigger lucky if you don't get a bullet to the head. I wet my panties that night that's how terrified I was. After all these beatings he would say I made him beat me then he would make me have sex with him. Of course I had to do it, if I didn't he would beat me again. I had bald spots in my scalp from the numerous times he pulled my hair out. I had to get my hair braided because the middle was so bald. I eventually learned how to braid my own hair with extensions to cover the bald spots. I was truly a battered woman. He would use any thing he could get his hands on to hit me with. He hit me with a chair. On several occasions he hit me with the broom. The stick and the bristles. He hit me with a baseball bat across my back. The night he hit me with the bat I screamed so loud from the pain that the neighbors called the cops. The cops came and again he got arrested. When I opened the door the cops the saw my eye which was almost swollen shut. I could barely see out of it. The cops roughed him up and this time I was kind of glad. They threw him on the floor real hard because he was resisting arrest, yelling at me the whole time talking about see what you making them do. I again went to court and the judge released him again with a second amended order of protection. 4ᵗʰ order of protection. We had to go back to court in 30 days. Back then the Domestic Violence laws weren't like they are today. Now the courts are a lot stricter with Domestic Violence and with great cause, because so many women have died due to being beat to death and killed by their abuser. Back in the days the judge would release the abuser from the court with an order of protection they would come back to court in a certain amount of time. He knew how the system worked so he would come right back home and beat me up again. I could have left but I really was not suppose too sleep in my mom so I just stayed with him because this was my home. After he was released from court, he came home and threatened everyone in the building telling them he is going to find out who called the cops on him. He was yelling that they are going to have to move out the building. When I tell you his fool was crazy I truly mean he was crazy. My daughter would to his mom house for the weekends which was good to give my mom a break. His mother wanted my daughter stay with her but my mom had temporary custody through the court.

Chapter 24

Running for My Life

On Easter Sunday his mom invited me to go to church with the family. We had been talking about going to church all month and because I didn't have any church clothes she brought me a beautiful dress. I was excited because I hadn't been to church since I was a little girl so I really wanted to go to church. His mom called the house too wake me up for church that morning. I guess I was too excited because he told me I couldn't go to church. I asked why. He said because he said I couldn't go. I told him but I'm going with your mother. He still said no. I was angry because he know we had been talking about this for weeks. Well, I decided I was going to take a stand and do what I wanted to do which was go to church. He left the house to go to the store so I took a quick shower and put on the dress she had brought me weeks before. I was determined to go to church. When he came back from the store I was almost ready to walk out the door. He waited all the way until I got dressed and started beating me up. He punched me in my face and head butted in my forehead. I felt like I was going to pass out he hit me so hard. He kicked me in my stomach and spit on me as always. My forehead started bleeding from the small cut he kept reopening whenever he head butted me which was quite often. I had blood on my dress. I was pissed because I really liked this dress. His mom took me to Graham Avenue the week before and brought this dress and a pair of shoes for church. He already knew we had plans to go to church. He went in the bathroom to get a rag to wipe blood off of my face. Which was what he always did after he beat me up trying to act so concerned. He wiped the blood off my face as I lay across the bed crying, wishing I didn't have to live like this anymore. He went to take his morning shower as he did every morning before he hit the streets to sell his drugs. When I heard the water running I got up off the bed and ran as fast as I could to the front door. I lightly opened the door and closed it very gently. Once I was out of the house I knew I had only a few minutes before he would realize I wasn't there and would come after me. I decided to run to his mom house which was the only person I knew on that side of Brooklyn. I didn't take a dime with me not even my pocketbook I just ran out the door. My adrenaline was pumping. I was running as fast as I could. I notice people were looking at me, cars were stopping to let me run across streets. I though people were looking because I had blood on my dress a cut on my forehead. I realized I didn't have any shoes on my feet. I ran out the house without anything on my feet. I had on panty hose that I put on with my dress. I was barefooted running through the street. I was turning up blocks running for my life cutting across streets. I ran through the schoolyard not taking any direct path. I didn't want him to catch me before I got to his mother house. His mom lived about 15 blocks from us and I was determined to get there alive. I can't even tell you how I felt running for my life not knowing if he was behind me or going to cut me off from another direction. I never looked back, I never looked over my shoulders, I never stopped for cars, I just ran and ran and ran until I got to this mom building. I ran upstairs to the second floor to their apartment and started banging on the door. I was out of breath and couldn't even talk. When his sister opened the door I literally fell into the apartment crying and screaming. I blurted out he's coming he going to get me please hide me. I was crying and screaming at the same time. They gave me some water and was trying to ask me what happened. I was trying to tell them what happened but I literally could not talk because I was frightened and out of breath. I was hyperventilating. All of a sudden he starts banging on the door and can you believe they let him in. He came charging right at me and started beating me up right where I was sitting at on the couch right in front of everybody. He had his gun on him as always but he didn't pull it out but I felt the heaviness of it when he was on top of me. He was punching me in my face like I stole something from him. His mom, sisters and stepfather were all trying to pull him off of me. Once they finally got him off of me his mother asked what happened. He was standing there and in a rage. Everyone was standing around like they were afraid to tell him he was wrong. I tried to explain through tears and fear because he was still standing there looking at me. I told his mom I got dressed to come to church with you guys and he beat me up. I had to run for my life. Can you believe his mother had the nerve to say to us you guys need to work this out. WHAT!! Here I am in your living room a bloody mess, forehead busted open, lip busted, face swollen from him just beating me like a rag doll and my feet were filthy and she had the nerve to say WORK IT OUT!!! But God, again God was covering me, yet another moment in my life that I didn't realize I was being covered by God. His Grace is so sufficient. M y feet could have been all cut up from glass as I ran approximately 15 blocks with no shoes on my feet trying to escape from this maniac. I bet if the shoe was on the other foot and I was her daughter she would not under any circumstances have told me to work it out with my abuser. But, because he was her son she felt we should try and work it out. Now this is in no way to down her or talk about her. If she ever reads my book I don't want her to take this personal but I have to keep it real. No mother is going to tell their daughter or son to stay with someone that's beating them. But, let me also say that I loved and still love her to this day. When I was down and out and had no one in my corner, she was there to help me pick up the pieces and put my broken dysfunctional life back together. She always showed me love. She fed me, clothed me, put a roof over my head, took care of my son as her own and took care of my daughter better than I could of at that time. I was a drug addict so I wasn't capable of taking care of myself let alone my children. She never asked me for anything and she loved me unconditionally. For this I will always love, respect and admire her. I love you Maureen. Saying I was a drug addict seems so harsh even to myself but the reality is anything that you are a prisoner to is an addiction. Drugs, Alcohol, Coffee, Caffeine, Nicotine, Sleeping pills and etc. Can all become addictive if used excessively and will become a habit that is a addiction. Ok, so back to my life before I get all emotional and cry on this computer keyboard. One thing I learned in my many lessons in life is, you never forget where you came from and you never forget those who helped you along the way. I have been truly blessed with genuine people in my life and for that I am forever humbled and grateful. May God always and continue to bless all those who made a profound impact in my life. I will mention them later. I went back home with him of course and again he was so sorry for beating me yet again. The sad part was he did this in front of his family and they didn't seem to have a problem with his behavior. I just think we were all afraid of him. He took care of my feet which were aching from running on the hard pavement. His sister gave me her slippers to wear. I didn't even want to put a shoe on my foot that is how bad they were aching. He gave me a bath and we had a great night. I knew it was just a matter of time before he would beat me again. Well of course I was right. We were getting high the next day which we never really stopped getting high we just wasn't doing it as often. He realized he was using more drugs then he was making money. He decided we should slowed down on getting high everyday which was ok with me since I had to give urine test when my caseworker requested me to. I had already decided I wanted to slow down on getting high. Eventually, I did plan to get my kids back from my mom. I knew she was tired working and taking care of my kids. I would go over there to see the kids but I really wasn't suppose too be there. We had to be careful that the caseworker didn't pop up. My son father was around a lot and I knew my daughter father was jealous of him. I tried to not be around when he was there. My family loved my son father way more then they liked my daughter father. I know that was because my son father was humble, kind, had a very good heart and was a caring person. My daughter father was arrogant, belligerent, rude, violent and people just didn't like him including me I loved him but I didn't like him. It felt strange to love someone who you didn't like, heck I didn't even understand it. I was at my mom house and my daughter father came over there. My daughter was drinking whole milk by then she was about 8months old.

Chapter 25

He Stabbed My Brother

My brother who I met Paul through, and mind you they were like best friends before I started messing with him, used some of my daughter milk to eat some cereal. I was arguing with my brother about drinking up my daughter milk and my daughter father involved himself in the argument. The argument escalated between them two. I tried to calm both of them down but they were pushing me out the way trying to get to each other. I went to put my daughter in her crib because they were about to fight. Next thing I knew my daughter father ran out the house. It happened so fast that no one in the house even saw what happened. My daughter father stabbed my brother in the stomach with a screwdriver that was sitting on the bookshelf by the front door. My brother started screaming he stabbed me, he stabbed me. He was holding his stomach as blood began to run down his shirt. My older brother, cousin and I ran out the door trying to catch this bastard but he was long gone. Thank you Jesus my brother was ok the screwdriver only cut the surface of his stomach. It could have been so much worse. My brother pressed charges against him. I was glad and mad at the same time. Glad because I was angry he stabbed my brother and mad because this was my daughter father and now he had the ultimate beef with my family. I was really caught between a rock and a hard place. I loved my brother but I loved and was in fear of my daughter father. Love on both levels but two different kinds of love. No one on my blocked that I grew up on liked my daughter father which was St. Johns Place. He got into some mess with a guy that I grew up with on the block. I remember so clearly the day this happened. I was pregnant with my daughter about 6 month. Paul and my homeboy had this feud which had been going on for some time. This particular day we were having our block party. I was outside cooking hamburgers and hot dogs on my mom grill. We were having a BBQ for the block party. Paul and my friend started arguing. I was far away so I couldn't hear what they were saying but I could tell by their demeanor that they were in a heated argument. Paul walked away from my friend so I thought the argument was over. Well wrong I was. Paul went in my mother house, took a pair of scissors and put them in his back pocket. He came back outside like everything was ok. My good friends father who was the block association president had organized a baseball game so everyone who was about to play were standing in the street. My homeboy was getting ready to play so he was standing in the crowd. Everyone was excited as the teams were being picked having a good time. I turned around just in time to see my daughter father pull out the scissors from his back pocket. All of a sudden my daughter father went running towards my homeboy with the scissors in his hand in a stabbing position. Running with the scissors straight for his head. My homeboy grabbed the bat from my friend father who had the bat in his hand and swung it as hard as he could to stop Paul from stabbing him. All I heard was a LOUD CRACK which was the bat coming in contact with my daughter father head. He hit him in the head like he was a professional ball player. The force of the impact knocked my daughter father to the ground. My friend commenced to beating Paul in the head and all about the body with the bat. I stood in shock as others tried to stop him. I surly wasn't going to get in between them I was pregnant. I thought Paul was dead because he wasn't moving at all. It was pure chaos after that. Kids were crying, people were running all over the place, adults were moving their kids out of the street. I heard people saying call the ambulance but I was frozen still in a state of shock at what had just happened. The Fire department was the first to arrive their Fire station is located on the next block still to this day. People had put towels Paul's head I guess to comfort him he was bleeding from his ear and he had a lot of abrasions and bruises. The Fire men put some smelling salt under his nose and he started coming to but he was out of it. The cops and the Ambulance finally arrived. They were asking what happened but no one wanted to talk, because as I stated no one liked my daughter father so they all felt it was good for him. They put him in the ambulance and of course I had to go with him to the hospital. I really didn't want to go, I wanted to stay at the block party plus I had my mom grill and when this happened I had food cooking on it. I knew I had to go with him to the hospital because in the event he did survive I would get beat by him for not being there. At the hospital they stabilized him and I told him what had happened. The first thing out of his mouth was I am going to kill him. The moment he said it I knew he meant it. I knew I had to warn my homeboy before any more blood was shed. He had a mild concussion and the doctor wanted to admit him overnight for observation, but he refused to be admitted. He decided to sign out against medical advice. He had all kinds of bruises swelling and abrasions on his face plus his body was all bruised up. I might be wrong to say this but I was like good for him he deserved every hit he got. He use to beat the crap out of me and now look at him all beat up in the Emergency Room. KARMA. After he was discharged we went home and I told him I had to go back to my mom house to clean up the stuff I left outside. We were in the hospital for a few hours so I knew the block party was still going on. He decided to go to his mom house so she could clean him up with her homemade remedies. When I got on the block my homeboy sister who I am still friends with to this day came up to me and asked me was Paul ok. I think people thought he was going to die that's how bad it was but I told her he left the hospital against medical advice. I needed to see my homeboy so I could tell him that my daughter father planned on killing him. When I finally saw my homey I warned him about what Paul said about killing him. He apologized to me for hitting him with the bat, but I told him he had to do what he had to do because if the shoe was on the other foot he would have stabbed him with the scissors. I'm glad he didn't kill him because I didn't want a dead baby father. I didn't want Paul to be in jail for killing him either so God took control of that situation. Again I did not know the favor of God was covering me. Paul stayed away from my neighborhood for a while. I figured he was embarrassed and didn't want everyone to see his face. My homey was walking around with his gun because he knew my daughter father always carried a gun and that he threatened to kill him. There was a lot of tension on the block for a little while. I never stopped speaking to my home boy I knew he had to defend himself and to this day we are still friends. My brother felt kind of bad for my daughter father so he didn't pursue the charges against him for stabbing him with the screwdriver. I was a glad because I didn't want him to have this ongoing feud with my family. Things started to get a little better between Paul and me. I was there to take care of him while he was hurt and I think he began to appreciate me. He hadn't hit me in a while and I was really doing good not getting high. One day he went out to sell his drugs and I noticed it was pass his time to come home. He normally stopped selling drugs at a certain time and came straight home. I was use to his schedule he stuck to his daily routine. The precinct called me in the wee hours of the morning because he ended up getting locked up on a drug charge. I had to verify to the officer his address and date of birth. I went to court the next day and the judge gave him a bail. I called his partner which is what he told me to do if he was ever arrested. His partner bailed him out. He had already been arrested a couple of times for drugs and domestic violence. Paul was very insecure and always thought I was cheating on him. I guess when you are taking drugs you're always in a state of paranoia. If he even remotely thought I was cheating he would beat me up. I could be totally innocent but that did not matter at all, if he thought it then it was true and that was that.

Chapter 26

It Only Gets Worse

One day I was hanging out with my friends, he thought I was cheating so when I got home he made me take off my panties so he could smell my private parts. I told him that wasn't necessary because I would not cheat on him. He told me if he smelled anything he was going to hurt me or if he smelled soap which would have meant I washed up when I finished having sex. This man was a fool. I cannot tell you how humiliated I felt to have this man make me open my legs so he could inspect my private area and he was dead serious. I was afraid that even though I didn't do anything he would accuse me anyway to have a reason to beat on me, luckily that night wasn't any violence. There was another time when he did beat me because I broke my 9 pm curfew he had set for me. Here I am a grown women and this man gave me a curfew. My momma didn't even tell me when to come and go when I was in her home. I couldn't figure out how I was allowing this man to dictate when I could come and go, but I listened because I didn't want to be hit. My friends would say beep him and ask him can you stay out a little longer but when I would beep him he wouldn't call me back so I knew I better go home. I hated it because I wanted to stay outside with my friends but I knew no one would be there to stop him when he jumped on me. One of my best friends use to tease me and say "go home house wife" I use to laugh but deep down inside it hurt to have to live like this. No one really understood what I was dealing with. The fear of going home and being beat without even provoking the situation. One incident really broke my heart and sticks with me today. All of my beatings stick with me and always will be at the back of my head. A true reminder of what I survived. We moved yet again. This was our fourth time moving in two years. I think he liked to stay on the move so people wouldn't get to use to him being in one place. That is the life of a drug dealer. You can't trust anyone so you keep on moving. We were now living on Dean Street. I realized we kept moving because as a drug dealer you always feel like you are being watched, or someone is scheming on you. Planning to rob you, kill you or report you to the police. My daughter father made enemies any place we lived so he always slept with his gun under his pillow and one eye open. Which had me leery to get good sleep also. People didn't like him because he had a nasty attitude. It was a known fact that he beat me constantly and that also cause a lot of dirty looks and stares when we would come and go from where we lived. I know a lot of people were looking at me and wondering why is she still with him. They were right, but no one really understood why I was still with him. I don't think I even understood why I was still with him. Moving to this new place was a good thing because no one knew us. It was a fresh start with new neighbors. Maybe he wouldn't be so abusive around new neighbors. Wrong. The beatings followed me. I thought, a new place, a fresh start but nope he was still the same person. While living on Dean Street, he was still selling drugs even though he still had open court cases. I don't think he even cared that he was back and forth to court for the previous cases he had. He kept selling drugs like it was legal. He had a couple of workers who sold drugs for him. It was easier and safer to have someone doing the dirty work for you. One worker he had was an addict himself. He smoked crack and he would constantly short his money. I believe he liked having people who were addicted to drugs sell for him, that way he could pay them in crack and not cash. One day his worker came to the house and was short some money. I already knew my daughter father was going to give him the business so I stayed out of his way. I learned to stand clear of him when he wasn't in the best of moods. I didn't want him taking his anger out on me as he always does. So, this particular day we were sitting on the stoop of the house we lived in. This was a four story brownstone we lived in and I loved it. I was back on my side of town, close to my family and friends. When his worker came up he asked him for the money he made for the night before from selling his drugs. The worker started to explain some story about what happen last night. I saw the look in my daughter father eyes so I knew it was about to be on. He told me to go upstairs and get his bat. My heart started to race because I knew he liked hitting people with his bat so I knew the worker was in for a beat down. I didn't want to go get the back but I had no choice. When I came back downstairs he had the man hands on the ground. He was stepping on his hands and telling him this is what happens when you steal from me. The man was actually sitting on the ground in our front yard and my daughter father made him stretch his hands out on the ground as he was standing and grinding his sneakers into his hands. The man wasn't even crying, he just looked like he was in shock. I felt so sorry for him. I could not believe that he would do this right in public, in the front yard in front of all to see. He look the bat from me and told me to go upstairs. I kind of wanted to stay to see what he was going to do but of course I ran back up the stairs. Before I could get back up the stairs he hit him in the legs with the bat. All I remember was the man crying out in such pain that it made tears come into my eyes. I went upstairs feeling sorry for the man. I knew my daughter's father wouldn't stop until he saw blood or was satisfied the beating was enough. When he came upstairs I asked him what happened just to break the tension. He said he sent him away. I heard the siren of an ambulance. I knew it was worse then he said it was. A few days later my neighbor told me she saw everything from her front window. Paul beat him about the body with the bat in his legs and punched him in his face a few times with his fist. When the seller got to the corner he couldn't walk some people called the ambulance for him and he went to the hospital. I was afraid he was going to tell the police what happen but no police ever came to arrest Paul for that assault. The seller was too afraid to tell on Paul. Believe it or not two weeks later he came right back to sell drugs for Paul. I couldn't really say anything to him about why he would come back to sell drugs for Paul after he beat him, after all I was a victim of his abuse as well. Every now and then to this day I run into him if I pass on Nostrand Avenue. Unfortunately he is still on drugs. One Friday I was hanging out with my friends on St. Johns where my still lived and I got home about an hour late. I figured I would have to have sex with him to make up for coming home late. When I got home he was already mad and I knew I was in trouble. He asked me why was I late before I could answer him he kneed me in my stomach. I curled over and grabbed my stomach and he punched me in my head. I ran as always to cower in the corner into a fetal position to protect my face he grabbed me by my hair and commenced to punching me about my body. He threw me on the bed and took the 2by4 piece of wood from under our bed, this is where he kept it easy access to hit me with. This was one of this weapons of choice to use on me. He hit me so hard in my leg I thought the stick broke in half, I screamed out in so much pain. I have never felt such pain in all the beatings I have received from him. This felt like the worse.

Chapter 27

My Friend Gets Hurt Because of Him

There was a neighbor Mr. Jay, who living directly next door to us. He was an older man in his early 60's. Where our bed was that was his wall to his bedroom room, he started banging on the wall. I guess he heard the beating which I'm sure wasn't the first time he heard me getting beat. Since being there in the new place just a few weeks he had hit me at least 3 times. My daughter father banged back on the wall. This was a whole new place we were living in, these neighbors didn't know our history of domestic violence so they wasn't with this fighting and cussing which was good for me. He starts cursing at the top of his lungs about people better mind there business unless they wanted some of what I was getting. He wanted the neighbors to hear him. That was his motto always trying to bully and put fear in people. I could barely walk for a few days. I had the biggest bruise across my whole right thigh. It was so ugly and discolored that I thought I would have to go to the hospital. He called his self being nice to me which was always the case when he beat me up. I had a problem with this because he only showed love to me when he saw the effects of his abuse. I went to my mom house a few days after the beating and my mom noticed I was limping. She asked me what was wrong and I told her about the beating so said let her see my leg when I pulled down my pants and showed her my leg she started crying. I didn't even realize how much worse it had gotten. Over time the bruise had gotten darker and it looked as though it got even bigger. My mom grabbed her Kodak instant camera and took pictures of my leg. She wanted me to call the cops on him but I was too afraid of what he would do to me. After I left my mom house that day I went to hang out with my friends. They also noticed I was limping and of course they wanted to know what happened this time. I pulled down my pants and showed them my leg and they were so shocked. They knew I was being abused and they saw my black eye, busted lip but nothing to this extent. My leg was bruised. One of my closest and good friends was so upset that she said you need to leave him and come stay with me. I wanted to get away I was really tired of being beat so I agreed to come stay with her. Being that the kids were still with my mom and now my daughter was with his mom I only had to worry about myself. The reason my daughter was now with his mom was because my mom was working and taking care of my two nieces and my two children. It was just a bit much on my mom so my daughter father asked could we take my daughter to his mom so that way it wasn't too much on my mom. We spoke to the social worker on my case and she agreed to let my daughter go. I didn't mind because my daughter was his mom's first grandchild so she could get the attention she needed. I had decided that I would take her up on the offer to stay with her. A couple of my friends decided to help me go move my stuff out of his house. I say his house because everything I owned he brought everything in the house he brought and he paid the rent and all the bills. So technically it was his house and I was fine with that to tell you the truth. Two of my close friends agreed to come help me. I warned them and I express warned them that we should take the cops with us because I knew he was a fool. They both felt that he would not do anything because they were there with me. I again expressed that we should take the police with us because I know this man or I thought I knew this man like a book. Again they insisted we don't need the police. So we walked from St. Johns to Nostrand to move my stuff out which I was only taking clothes which was all I owned in the house anyway. The closer we got to my house, I repeatedly kept telling them we need to take the cops with us and they still didn't listen to me. They figured he wouldn't do anything to me in front of them. They figured because he knew them and liked them as my friends that he would be cool. Well I knew totally different and I knew it wouldn't be a good idea to go without the police but they wouldn't listen to me. When we got to the house I rung the bell instead of using my keys, I wanted him to know I wasn't alone. As we made our way up the stairs, now, let me just say I walked up and down these stairs every day, we lived on the third floor with a walk in off the street basement so it was really equivalent to living on the fourth floor. No fire escape because it's a brown stone but we did have a sprinkler system in the hall way on each floor. There were 18 steps per each flight of stairs and there were two flights of stairs to get upstairs to my place. I was leading the way my girlfriends were behind me and the girlfriend who said I could stay with her was last coming up the stairs. As we got to the top of the stairs almost by my door he opened the apartment door. When he opened the door he stepped into the hallway and pulled his 9mm gun out from behind his back. He pointed it up towards the hallway ceiling as though he was taking the safety off, which I know he always kept the safety on because he slept with the gun under his pillow most of the time. When my girlfriends and I saw the gun we all screamed and turned to run down the stairs. My girlfriend who I was moving in with was the last one to come up the stair jumped down the whole entire flight of stairs and landed on her feet. My other girlfriend and I ran down the stairs behind her, we didn't know if this fool was going to shoot at us or what we just ran as fast as we could. We didn't stop running until we were on Bergen St. and Bedford Ave which is about 4 blocks away. When we stopped running my girlfriend who jumped down the stairs fell to her knees she was crying we were all crying. She realized that she could not stand back up on her feet. We found a stick in the garbage and we had to help her walk back home. She was in so much pain but we thought it was just because she jumped down the flight of stairs. I felt really bad because I knew this was my fault. They were trying to help me out and look what happened to her. When we got back on the block everybody was asking what happened and as we told them they started acting like it was my fault because she was helping me. I had to defend myself and tell everyone that I told them we should take the cops with us but they didn't want to listen to me. Well of course no one saw it that way all they were focused on was the fact that he pulled a gun on us and her foot was messed up. All of a sudden he pulls up in a cab as I was standing there talking to everyone and he called me to come to the cab. I was scared to go to the cab but I thought he had his gun on him. I didn't want him to shoot into the crowd which he would have done because he was just that crazy. I walked over to the cab and he told me I better get in the cab right now. I didn't want to and I told him I wasn't going back home with him he showed me his gun and said you got 1 second to get your butt in this cab. Of course I did as I was told I didn't want him to cause a scene out there. He would have dragged me in the cab by my hair. I never even went back over to my friends to tell them I was leaving I just got in the cab and we pulled off. I didn't even look back because I knew they were looking at the cab and thinking did she really just get in the cab with him. What they didn't know was that he showed me the gun so I had no choice but to go with him. Right before this incident happened I was going out with some of my girlfriends and this same girlfriend who got hurt was with us. He saw me get into a cab with them to go to the club and he chased the cab down. We were all yelling at the cab driver to please run the light because if he would have caught that cab I know he would have beat me right on the spot. Luckily the cab driver was able to get away from him. I felt like everyone was wrong for feeling I was responsible for my friend getting hurt. I truly felt hurt and bad for what happened to her but also I kept telling them we needed to take the police with us to move my stuff. She ended up having to go to the hospital she had a fractured ankle. She ended up with a cast on her leg for months. I felt so bad. She stopped speaking to me after that but I think it was really because I ended up going right back to him the same night this happened, but no one understood I was terrified of him. I knew what he was capable of doing to me if I tried to leave him. Praise God that my girlfriends and I are still friends to his day. That night he told me if I ever tried to leave him again he make sure no one ever found me. I truly believed him. All of my friends were upset with me that I went back to him. I was upset myself! My family was upset with me it was like everyone turned their back on me and I felt so alone. He was the only one who I had in my corner and that wasn't a good thing because he was my abuser.

Chapter 28

A Fresh Start or So I Thought

One of my best friends was working at the Board Of Education. She offered to help me get a job there with the temp agency she worked with. I was so excited because the only jobs I ever had were Wendy's Mc Donald's Burger King and Young World dept. I did work for this two different banks but they were very short positions only a couple of months. In all six of those jobs I probably lasted two years in total because I didn't like to listen or take orders from anyone. I also had a taste of the drug dealing life so that money was pennies to me. I was excited about the opportunity to work in a real job with paperwork and a computer. I wasn't very computer literate but they taught you everything you needed to learn. I told him I was going to the agency to get a job and he told me he didn't want me to work that he would take care of me. I told him in order for me to get the kids back I needed to have a job to show the judge. So he reluctantly agreed to let me work. He told me straight up I want you home barefoot and pregnant. I thought it was cute for him to tell me this but then reality set in that I would be barefoot pregnant and abused. I went to the agency and they assigned me to 131 Livingston St. My best friend worked on the 3rd floor and I worked on the second floor. I was totally drug free now, I hadn't gotten high in weeks and I didn't want to do it anymore. I realized that it wasn't doing me any good and it was keeping me from having my kids. I liked the job I had and he seemed to be ok with me working. Well that was short lived, one day he decided he wanted me to stay home with him and I told him I had to go to work. He waited until I was fully dressed and threw a whole pot of water on me. I still left and went to work dripping wet luckily it was summer time. When I met my friend at the train station which we use to meet up every morning, she looked at me and said you can't be serious I know he didn't throw water on you, I just looked at her and said yes he did but I still left to go to work. It actually got worse, he went from throwing water to sorrel and juice on me. Whatever was in the refrigerator that he could grab he would throw it on me. He thought I wasn't going to go to work sticky or stained but I would still go to work. One day I came home from work and he was in a very bad mood. He had the drugs out on the table and I knew that was a trick to get me back addicted but I wanted no parts of drug use any more. I was doing so good working, I felt like I had control over my life again. I didn't want any parts of drugs anymore using or selling. He told me he wanted me to bag up the drugs. I told him I didn't want to touch the drugs. I know how the temptation is so strong even just touching it can set you back to using. He got upset with me and started telling me I think I am better now that I was working and I think I'm too good to help him anymore. He started calling me all kinds of horrible names and I knew already next would be the hitting. Well yes he sure did punch me right in the stomach I curled over and grabbed my stomach and he punched me in the back of my head I cried out from the pain.

Chapter 29

My New Neighbors

My neighbor started banging on the wall because he heard me crying. Paul started cursing him out through the wall and I heard my neighbor yelling back but I couldn't make out what he was saying. Paul continued hitting me and I was yelling why are you hitting me what did I do. Before you know it there was a bang at the door not a knock but a bang. He at first wouldn't answer the door but the banging would not stop. He told me to answer the door and get rid of who it was. As I went to the door and asked who all I heard was "Police are you ok". I said through the door I am fine. One of the officers said can you open the door we need to see and talk to you. I cracked the door just a little and the officer said there was a report made that there was someone being beat in the apartment. I lied as usual and told the officer that everything was fine. He asked me could he look at me and I opened the door a little wider. I told him I was fine. One officer flashed his flash light in my face to see if I had any bruises on me which I didn't but I was a little red in the face. The other officer was writing and he finished writing me a long piece of paper to sign. I asked what it was he explained it was a report that they were there to investigate a Domestic Violence incident. I needed to go to the court to get an official report. I thanked them and they again asked me was I ok and I again said yes. After they left my daughters father went banging on the neighbors door and threatened him because he felt he was the one who called the cops. I was truly glad he did. My neighbor wasn't backing down but I know my daughter father would hurt him because my neighbor was an older man. My neighbor told him that my building was a quiet building and they wasn't use to the loud arguing and fighting. Paul told him to mind his business the more they argued the worse it got. The next thing I know my daughter father pushed him so hard that he fell to the floor. He started yelling he is going to call the cops and have my daughter father arrested. He ran in his house and called the cops. Paul left before the cops came. When the cops came back they banged on my door but of course Paul had already left the house. The cops told my neighbor to call them when he returned and they would lock him up for assault. Paul came back in the wee hours of the morning. The next day he went and knocked on my neighbor door and told him he saw when the cops came, he was standing on the next block watching. He told him he could give him something to forget about what happened. Well to my surprise my neighbor was getting high so my daughter father gave him some drugs and money to forget everything and it was forgotten. Now the person I thought would be my protector turned out to be my nightmare. He was on crack. All Paul had to do was pay him off with drugs or money and he would turn a blind eye to my cries for help. Luckily things were calm in the house for a little while. I guess my daughter father didn't want to push his luck. There are four apartments on my floor and the lady at the far end of the hall really disliked my daughter father. She didn't like the way he treated me and anytime she saw him she would give him dirty looks. He told me she didn't like him which I already knew that because she told me she didn't like him. One day she asked me were we married and I told her no. She asked me why I allow myself to go through the abuse. I didn't even know she knew he was beating me but then again it wasn't like he was quiet when he went on his tyrants against me. I was embarrassed when she was talking to me. She was much older than I was old enough to be my momma. She told me she left her husband for the same reason and that it never stops it only get worse. Of course I wasn't trying to hear that but I did listen. He caught me standing in the hall talking to her one day and he told me to stay away from her. He felt he could not trust her and if she knew he was dealing drugs he felt she would call the cops on him. Though he wasn't selling drugs from the house he did bag up the drugs in the house. Plus he had all the paraphilia in the house, Weight scales, Baking soda, Glass cook pipes, razor blades, crack capsules, crack bags etc. One day she was sweeping the hallway on our floor and they ended up getting into it. I really don't remember what it was about but he was very superstitious and didn't want her sweeping by our door. She told him off and let him know she wasn't scared of him and she had sons his age and she would call them if he messed with her. I really liked her and I was sad this happened. I knew once he had it out for you it was going to be all out war. One day I went out for drinks after work with my best friend and some coworkers. When I got home I was a little tipsy and feeling great. I didn't really hang out much in professional circles so I really enjoyed myself. It was different from being around my neighborhood friends. He was upset as always talking about we was supposed to go to his mom house to see my daughter. I asked him why he didn't beep me and he thought I was being funny so he slapped the wind out of me. I started yelling telling him I am tired of him hitting me and I wanted my neighbors to know it was about to hit the fan. He started telling me I was disrespecting him and I knew better then to talk back to him. Remember, as I told you earlier in the book that I could not suck my teeth, mumble under my breath or even roll my eyes without him feeling it was a direct disrespect to him. He picked up his belt from off the bed and began to hit me all over my body with the belt. Like he was beating a child who had misbehaved. I was fully dressed but I could feel each hit of the belt. My legs, my arms, my face, my back where ever the belt made contact I could feel the stinging. I was trying to crawl under the bed to get away from him but he flipped the bed over and continued beating me. All I could do was lay there when he was done. My body was extremely sore and aching. I knew I had whelps marks all over my body from the belt. I didn't want to see myself in the mirror I knew I looked a mess. I don't know which one of my neighbors called the cops but they came banging on our door. He answered the door and began to tell the cops they had no business coming to his door that he did not call the cops. They asked was there anyone else in the home and he tried to close the door in their face but they pushed the door and put him in handcuffs. I came to the door when I heard all the commotion and he was telling them to get the every curse you could think of off of him. They arrested him and as they were talking him down the stairs the neighbors were in the hallway and they were happy to see him getting arrested. I tried to ask the cops what were they arresting him for, one of the officers told me there was a domestic violence in progress report and when they came to talk to him, he threatened the officers and tried to close the door on the officers hand and foot that was in the doorway. The officer wrote a report for the domestic violence and gave me the copy. I tried to deny there was anything going on and the officer said look at your face. When I looked in the mirror I had red marks all over my face. The belt did hit me in the face and he slapped me when I fell on the floor. The cop asked me if I wanted to go to the hospital but of course I refused. They took him to the 77 precinct and honestly I was happy for a night of peace. I knew they weren't going to let him out without seeing the judge because he had a history with the police. I think him and the cops were on a first name basis that's how many times they had incidents with him. He had run-ins with the cops in the street and incidents when they came to the house. He didn't respect the police and I remember several times he would tell the police if you didn't have that gun I would whip your tail. Of course he didn't say it that nice but I must. There was a time when I was really ready to leave him and move on with my life. He went to court for that incident and was given 30 days in jail. It wasn't much time but I would have a little bit of peace. I decided to move out while he was in jail. They sent him to the jail called The Briggs on Flushing Avenue in Brooklyn. He had money in the house so I paid the landlord the next two month's rent so he had a roof over his head when he came out.

Chapter 30

Moving on with my Life

I packed my clothes and I moved in with my two childhood friends they were sisters. I was afraid to take anything out of the house like a TV because I didn't buy it. They had an apartment way across town on Gunther Place in Bedford Stuyvesant. This was a little small block that if you didn't know was there you would miss it. I was grateful they offered me a place to stay and no one knew where they lived except us close friends. I told my mom that I was leaving him but I didn't want to tell too many people because everyone can't be trusted to keep my secret. My mom had by this time moved off of St. Johns to Lefferts place a few blocks away. My friends had a 3 bedroom apartment so I had my own room. We shared the bills and the rent three ways. I was happy for a fresh start. I went to see him in the jail but I didn't let anyone know. I didn't tell him I left I let him think I was still in the apartment. I did tell him I paid two month's rent which was ok with him. One think I can say was he had thousands of dollars in the stash speaker and he wasn't a cheat man. He didn't have a problem giving me money he just wanted to control me. I didn't go hanging out in the neighborhood I grew up in because I knew he would be looking for me when he came out of jail. I was thriving and very happy in my job. About a month had passed and I knew he would be getting out of jail any day. I hadn't been back to see him since the last time. I probably visited him about three times while he was in that jail. I was correct people told me he was around the hood asking for me. Luckily my peeps were faithful to me and didn't tell him anything. I went to work that Monday and of course he came up to the job and tried to beat me up. He came into the building and came upstairs to the second floor where I worked. I don't know how he managed to get passed the Officer at the front desk but nothing shocked me with him. My cubicle was towards the back of the office by the window so I didn't see when he pushed the door open. He asked my coworker who desk is by the front door for me. He had never been upstairs to my office so he didn't know exactly where my desk was located. I'm sure if he did he would have walked up to my desk and assaulted me right there. My coworker yelled over said there was someone there to see me. I looked from around mu cubicle but I didn't see anyone. I got up and went into the hallway and he grabbed me and began to punch me in my face. My director heard the commotion and she and several of the offices employees came running into the hallway. He started cursing everybody out and said some words I can't even repeat. They start yelling call the security guard. I guess they though that would scare him but they didn't know him like I knew him. He wasn't afraid of no officer especially one who worked for the Board Of Education and didn't carry a gun. He said to me to give me my coat that he had brought me. I love my beautiful coat and I couldn't believe he would take the coat off my back in the middle of the winter. I told him I couldn't give him the coat because I didn't have anything else to wear. The officer came upstairs and told him he had to leave. He turned and acted like he wanted to fight the officer so they called the cops. My Director told him he had to leave the building and he said he wasn't leaving without his coat. My director told me to give him the coat and she would give me something to wear. I reluctantly gave him my coat with tears in my eyes. I could not believe he was taking my coat off my back in the dead of winter. He made sure he left before the cops came. When they came the officer called me downstairs to speak to the cops. They asked me what happened and I told them the truth. My director came downstairs and told them she saw him assault me. She was so afraid for me I saw the fear in her eyes. The cops took a report I didn't really want them to but they had to because it happened on city property. The police gave me the same piece of paper I have seen numerous times the police report. My director was so afraid for me now she understood all the black eyes, busted lips and bruises in my face. She just hugged me and I felt such care and concern from her. She said to me I am going to see to it that you press charges in order for me to keep my job and make sure all the staff felt safe at work she was really concerned for my safety. My director gave me a sweater to wear and the police dropped me and my best friend at Dekalb Avenue train station. I kept looking out the window as we were driving in the cop car fearing that he saw me get in the cop car and he was following us. I did go to the court and get an Order of Protection this was my fifth. I never go back to court and keep them enforced which was what you had to do every six months to keep them active. When I got back to work, I had to give a copy to the school safety officer who was on post at the front desk when you enter the building. My daughter father was not allowed on the premises anymore. For about two weeks he left me alone. I didn't hear from him at all, he didn't beep my phone or call my job which I had my own extension on my desk. One day he came to my job and was waiting outside for me to come out. I didn't even see him it was my best friend who said look who standing across the street. I was afraid but he said he just wanted to talk. I agreed to go and talk with him in a public place. My friend left and we walked and sat on a bench to talk. He apologized as usual and promised he would never hit me again. I knew that wasn't true but I listened anyway. I really didn't want to get back together with him but I did want to keep the lines of communication open. I guess I was scared to totally cut him off number one my daughter still lived with his mother and number two I didn't want him to make me disappear if I left him. When I got home that night I told my friends that I hung out with him and they were upset with me. I understood that they cared about my safety and didn't want me to get hurt by him. I tried to explain that it was important for me to keep the lines of communication open. My friends made it very clear that he was not welcomed into the apartment and I agreed that it wasn't not even up for discussion. I didn't want him there either I didn't trust him. I met and started dating someone else for a short period of time but my heart was with my daughter father. I started seeing him again but I just didn't tell anyone. He wanted me to move back home but I wasn't ready to go back. My friends were mad at me because they knew every time I didn't come home I was with him and they were right. They would beep me and I wouldn't answer them which would make them worry about me. Eventually my friend told me I had to go they didn't want me there anymore and they were thinking about moving out of state. I was upset but deep down inside I was happy because I decided I wanted to go back home to my daughter father. I was only gone from him for a couple of months and I was missing him. Why? Why would I want to go back to him when he constantly abused me verbally and physically? I didn't even understand why I wanted to be with him. I believe when you are a victim of Domestic violence you become programmed, in fear of your abuser, so we feel it's better to stay and suffer then to leave and live in fear for the rest of your life. Of course that's just my opinion. My friends that I lived with stopped talking to me when I moved back in with my daughter father. When I looked at it I was losing friends because of him but I guess being young and immature I felt they were wrong not me. I don't think anyone understood what I was dealing with. I figured why stop speaking to me because I chose to stay with my baby daddy. I didn't judge them when they stayed with their boyfriends and they had problems. Granted they wasn't being beaten to a bloody pulp but he didn't always mean it. I was the cause some of the beatings. That's how a victim think that we did something to cause the beatings. We always try and justify the abuse, typical domestic violence syndrome I know it so well.

Chapter 31

Back to Torture

Once I moved back in the apartment on Dean Street, things seemed to be going ok. He stopped beating me and we were getting along. We would go out together which was something we rarely did. We had both stopped using drugs which was awesome. He seemed a lot calmer since he wasn't getting high. Well we weren't smoking crack anymore but we were smoking weed which was cool because it wasn't as bad a crack. I always smoked weed but when the crack came along it was a better high so it became more popular. Marijuana wasn't as addictive and it was normal to smoke weed. He stopped selling drugs and got a job with his friend who owned a Floor Scraping Company. He seemed a lot happier and he loved this job. He also knew he couldn't get into any more trouble. Things were a lot better and I felt like it was our first time meeting again. He was getting up going to work we would leave the house together things were great. One day I came home and he was in a really good mood. He cooked dinner and the house was nice and clean. I made sure I was on my best behavior and didn't want to do anything to ruin the mood he was in. there was a box on the table and I kept looking at it but I didn't want to ask him what was in the box. I figured if he wanted me to know he would have told me so I just chilled. I loved the fact that he loved and knew how to cook. We both could cook but he did his West Indian dishes and I specialized in my American dished so it was great. That night after dinner he came to the bed where I was laying and pulled out the box I saw on the table. In the box was the most beautiful diamond engagement ring. He asked me to marry him. I cried I was really shocked. I didn't know what to say but I knew better than to say no. Of course I said yes. We had a beautiful night after that we made passionate love better than we had in a long time. I couldn't wait to show off my ring. When I got to work the next morning my best friend was disgusted with me. She couldn't believe I was even considering marrying him. My director and co-workers looked at me in amazement that I even went back to him. But. At the time I didn't care what they thought, they didn't know my life or story but they did see me come to work all battered. Now they could put a face to his fist. I went around to my neighborhood showing off my ring to my friends and everyone was pissed with me. I felt that they were just jealous because none of them had an engagement ring on their finger. Of course I saved showing my ring to my family last because I knew they were going to give me the business and tell me off. I went to my mom house and when she saw the ring she begged me not to marry him. She told me I would be giving him papers to own me and if I think I was bad then just wait until I marry him. My mom actually had tears in her eyes. My sister, Brothers and Stepfather just looked at me and shook their heads. Nobody was happy for me not my family or my friends. I acted like I didn't understand why they wasn't happy for me but I knew exactly why because this was his way of really controlling me and beating me. Now he would have papers on me like my mom said. Thank God I didn't marry him I'm sure I would have regretted it to this day. Again that was the Grace and favor of God over my life making my decisions for me. I decided I had to think about if I wanted to marry him because no one would probably come to the wedding anyway. Of course I could not tell him this he would probably beat me senseless. So I wore the ring on my finger and acted like I was so happy. In all honesty, I was happy because I never been engaged before so it was exciting to wear the nice diamond ring. But, deep down inside that ring came with a lot of hurt, fear and pain. Once we got engaged he got even worse the old behavior slowly began to resurface. He started telling me I couldn't go out with my friends anymore he had to know my every move. I was tired of living this way but I put myself back in this situation. I had so many opportunities to leave and I actually left but I always made my way right back to the abuse. Now, I was losing family members, losing friends and losing myself all over again. I went to church with his mom a few times and I remember listening to the Pastor talk about "talk to God" "pray he hears you he will answer your prayers". I decided I wanted to talk to this God I hear so much about. I mean at this time in my life I didn't see anything that God was doing for me. I was going to so much in my young life that I didn't see any hope for a bright future. I had done been molested several times by several men, tried to commit suicide, Stabbed someone, kicked out of three schools, addicted to crack, beat, battered, abused so where did I fit in in Gods life. No one like me because I was making stupid decisions. The only person I thought loved me which was my daughter father I was petrified of. So what kind of future did I have left? Did I fit in anywhere? I was almost suicidal again but I loved living. I loved bring alive, I loved working, I loved my children, I just hated myself. I truly hated myself. I didn't like the person I was.

Chapter 32

Will God Hear Me After All I've Done

I had become hard and insensitive ready to fight at a drop of a hat. Now I was always like this but I did mature a lot when I became a mom but I saw the old way creeping back up in me. He was turning me into the person I was running from. The person I didn't want to be anymore. The person that just didn't care anymore rather she lived or died. I had to put a stop to this thinking this stinking thinking, this self-destructive behavior. I decided to look in the mirror and really see into my soul to see if there was just a little bit of life left. If I still had any fight left in me, if I even wanted to fight anymore. If I wanted to just lay down and give up go out like a chump and just give up. Well, I ain't never been no punk except when it came to my daughter father beating on me. But I always stood up for myself, went after what I wanted, so now I wasn't going to give up. I decided to take a stand and make some changes but I couldn't tell anyone I was going to talk to this God and see if he could help me.

Chapter 33

My Prayer even through the Storm

I decided I needed to talk to God in private so I use to go into my bathroom, turn on the water, get on my knees and ask God I would say 'God don't hurt him don't kill him but just take him out of my life". It felt good being on my knees in my own space talking to God. I liked it and decided I needed to do this more often. I began to say this prayer a couple times a month and I started to feel different about myself. I found something to believe in, something to look forward to. Praying was beautiful and it was my secret. I didn't share this with anyone manly because I didn't want anyone trying to discourage me from believing God will answer my prayer. I had not heard anyone really taking about God that much, I mean I ran in circles in the streets and we sure weren't praying before we got high or went into the clubs to shake our tails. It got so good the feeling of praying that I started saying it every week, "God don't kill him, don't hurt him, just take him out of my life" I even noticed that he wasn't beating me as much maybe a slap here or there but nothing as bad as before. I realized I could pray whenever I wanted to not just when he would beat me but in good times as well. I did it because I wanted an escape and I was too afraid of what he would do to me if I ever really left him. I wasn't really into praying at that time and felt like I didn't have a relationship with God. I knew God existed because I was raised to believe in God and we grew up to church. I loved the church we attended when we were growing up. Light house Church of Love and Peace in Brooklyn. I really didn't know anything about trusting or believing God but I was willing to give it a try I had become hopeless in my situation with him. I was now saying that prayer faithfully on my knees daily. I was not saved nor was I even thinking about getting saved. As a matter of fact I was just the opposite of a Christian I was a sinner. I was deep in sin Drinking, Drugging, Fighting, Cursing, Gossiping, having sex without marriage etc. I did not know how to pray the perfect prayer which I thought I had to pray a certain way in order for God to hear me. Not knowing that God want us to come to him just the way we are. For some reason whenever I prayed that prayer, I believed in my heart that God was going to answer me. I began to look forward to being away from my daughter father. The beatings weren't as frequent because I learned how to not trigger him off, though it was hard living like that not knowing what buttons you may push that would set him off. I have learned that abuse is never ok. Mental abuse, Physical abuse, Emotional abuse, Verbal abuse are unacceptable and should never be tolerated be it man or woman doing the abusing. It is not a form of love, it is a form of control, intimidation, inflicting fear on one. We confuse abuse as being loved by your abuser. We see this behavior as" well they love me so much that they don't want anyone else to have me". WRONG on so many levels. Love does not hurt, love surly don't hurt you physically. I'm not saying we aren't going to go through issues in relationships we may not like. I am saying love should not give you black eyes and busted lips. Love neuters you and builds you up not beat you and tear you down. I was learning these things as I opened my prayer life up and started being intimate with God. I have learned in this process that the abuser normally have a history of either going through some childhood trauma or even having been abused themselves. Hurt people tend to hurt people. I know this statement to be very true because I was hurt as a child and as I grew up I tended to hurt people. I was a broken child so I became a broken adult. I am a living testimony that this is very true. Only God can restore you back to that whole person. We have to let got and let God. I got home from hanging out with my friends this particular night and for some reason I felt like something was going to happen to me when I got home.

Chapter 34

A Feeling of Doom

A feeling of fear overcame me as I headed home. I was 1 minute late on my 9pm curfew but I didn't think much of it. Well, when I got in the house he was extra quiet and I knew that was a sign of trouble. I said hi and went to give him a kiss and he pulled away from me. He was in the kitchen cooking so I said to him what you cooking it smells good. Again he ignored me. This was not a good sign I thought, but I decided to play it cool. I was nervous because I felt something was going to happen. I began to take my clothes off being a quiet as I could so I wouldn't make him any madder. He called my name and I hurriedly replied yes. He said he wanted me to cook the rice. Now, this was warning number three that something was wrong, he knew I was terrible at cooking rice it either came out to sticky or to watery. Either way I knew he was setting the mood to beat me. I literally walked around on pins and needles because I knew it was just a matter of time before he was going to strike. I went into the kitchen and started to prepare the rice. I always put too much water in my rice so I tried to do it perfectly so he wouldn't get upset. I could never get the right water measurement which is the key to making perfect rice. After putting on the rice I went into the room to finish getting undressed. Something told me to keep my jeans on which one of the first things I do when I get in the house is take off my street clothes and put on something more comfortable. I decided for some reason I followed my mind. I went into the bathroom and turned on the water and began to pray and ask God as I always did "God don't hurt him don't kill him just take him out of my life". I swear I felt like finally my prayer was going to be answered. I had a different feeling when I prayed this time. A feeling of peace came over me. I came out the bathroom and I went over to the bed to sit down and he said check the rice. I went to check the rice and it looked like the water had cooked out so I thought it was done. I told him I think the rice is done and went and sat back down. He called me to come into the kitchen and when I walked into the kitchen he was tasting the rice with a spoon. I saw the look in his eyes that look of here comes trouble.

Chapter 35

Will I Live through This

I knew something was going to happen I just did not know what. All of a sudden he takes the whole pot of rice from off top of the stove and throws the pot against the wall yelling at me that the rice was sticky and berating me about how I can't do nothing right. Then all the abusive words and disrespectful names followed. He dragged me by my hair over to the rice all over the floor and on the wall. He threw me face first in to the rice that smeared down the wall and ordered me to clean it up with my hands. Of course you can't sweep up wet sticky rice because it will mess up the broom. As I was on my knees picking up the rice grains with my hands, he would walk over to me and kick me in the groin area. I cried out in pain because being on the floor already I felt the full force of the kick. He stood over me as I was picking up the rice so I knew the beating it wasn't over yet. After I picked up all the rice off the floor and wall he started yelling for me to wash the wall where the rice he threw stained the wall. I got a sponge and started to wash the wall but before I could finish he grabbed me by my hair and began to punch me in my face with a closed fist. He dragged me from the kitchen to the bedroom by my hair on my knees. I saw blood on the floor but I wasn't sure where it was coming from but I knew it was coming from somewhere on my body. My knees started burning so I realized the blood was coming from my knees. We had real wood floors and from dragging me my knees had big cuts on them marks I still have to this very day. I tasted blood in my mouth so I knew my lip was busted. As he was dragging me I'm crying and asking him to please stop what did I do? I heard him say these words very clearly 'YOU GONE DIE TODAY". He let my hair loose which freed me to get up off the floor. He went towards the big black music speaker he had in the room. Well this speaker was where he hid his drugs and guns. The front of the speaker was hollowed out he had a speaker sitting in the hole but if you looked inside there were no wires connected it was his stash spot. I knew when I saw him going towards the speaker that I was in serious trouble. The only thing in there that could hurt me was his gun and I knew he was going to get it. I peed on myself from the fear I felt as I jumped up off the floor and made a mad dash for the window. I decided I was not going to let this man kill me in this house and no one ever finds my body (God Forbid). As I got to the opened window because it was summer time so the window was already open. I was happy that I wouldn't have to waste time opening the window to jump out. I needed to get out the window before he caught me. We had a back apartment so our windows faced the backyard. We did not have a fire escape we lived in a brownstone and there were sprinklers in the hallways on every floor. We lived on the top floor which was considered the fourth floor because of the ground floor apartment. I knew when I went running for the window that I was going straight down to the concrete, no grass, no dirt, no flowerbed just a completely concrete backyard not even any patio furniture to break my fall. At this point I just didn't care anymore I was tired of getting beat. I didn't think of the consequences of what would happen to me or my body hitting the pavement below, all I cared about at that moment was escaping the brutality of his beatings. I made it to the window and I had my right leg out the window I was thinking if I land on my feet I might break my legs or feet but I might still live. I pulled my body around the window pain and was pulling my left leg out the window, before I could finish getting my leg out the window he grabbed me by my arm and started dragging me back into the window. He was screaming all kinds of profanities at me telling me "I was trying to make him kill me" and "I was trying to make them think he pushed me out the window". He began beating me even more for trying to kill myself and blaming him. I was baffled! How you trying to beat me to death but when I try to escape and jump out the window, you mad because you think I want them to think you pushed me out the window. Nevertheless, I ended up getting beat even more for trying to escape. He was stomping on me with his sneakers like I was an animal. I was on the floor in a fetal position my whole body ached, all I could do was pray in silence through my tears and sniffles God help me. He picked me up off the floor and laid me on the bed. He had some Epsom salt and warm water in a bowl and he began to wipe the blood off of my face. I didn't want to even see my body, I knew I was covered in many bruises. I just wanted him to get the hell away from me but of course I couldn't express this to him. When he was done cleaning me up, he started having sex with me. I was so repulsed that I felt sick. I started heaving like I wanted to vomit but nothing would come up. He let me go to the bathroom after he was one and I crumpled to the floor in tears when I looked at my face.

Chapter 36

Beat Battered Bloodied and Broken

My lip was busted, my ear was bleeding, I had lumps, bruises and swellings all over my body. This was the worst beating I had ever endured at this hands. I was in extreme pain and he had the nerve to climb on top of me and start whispering in my ear how much he loved me, why did I make him to this and how sorry he was. I wish I could have gotten off the bed and took his gun and shot him with it. That's what I wanted to do, I wanted to make him suffer just as he had made me suffer over the years, but I was afraid to even attempt something like that. Plus, I loved my freedom. I did not want to go to jail for killing this fool. The next day he left the house and I was talking to my mom on the phone. She could tell I was in a lot of pain. She asked me if he beat me again, I tried to lie but my momma wasn't no fool she knew exactly what was wrong. She said do you have some lye in the house. I told her no we didn't buy lye. She said you need to buy some and keep it under the sink where he won't see it, put on some water let it come to a boil and pour the lye in it, when he go to sleep prop the door open throw the water on him and run like hell. I laughed but I knew my mom meant business. My mom was a victim of Domestic Violence as well so she knew what I was going through. I thought about it after we hung up but I dismissed it because I thought what if he catches me, what if he dies then what will happen to me. I was confined to the house for a few days because I didn't want anyone to see my face also my body was still very sore from the beating. I could barely walk. I couldn't go to work. All I could do was go into the bathroom and ask God 'DON'T KILL HIM DON'T HURT HIM JUST TAKE HIM OUT MY LIFE' I tell you I said this faithfully constantly and daily. I was not a Christian. I did not go to church. I did not read the Bible. I did not pray on a regular basis other than to get away from him. I did not do anything for God to answer this prayer but I BELIEVED. I believed that one day he would be out of my life. I did not know how but I knew it would happen. I went to my mom's house a week later and I remember my mom had tears in her eyes when she saw the after effects of what he did to me. She pulled out her camera and began taking pictures of me. I felt so ashamed that my mom had to take pictures of my wounds. She said you need to have this documented. I finally was able to go back to my neighborhood and hang out with my friends and they all had tears in their eyes. I was limping and I just wasn't myself. I was broken physically maybe no bones were broken but I was wounded. My spirit was broken mentally the fear of knowing that this would be my life until it was finished. I just wanted to give up. This beating took so much out of me. I just didn't have the will to live anymore. I was an emotional wreck. I'm almost crying as I am writing this. I wanted to give up but I kept telling myself you have always been a fighter so why give up now. I would tell myself after all you've been through you can't give up now. I knew I could get him locked up for all the physical abuse and trauma my body had endured at his hands. Thank God my mom was a picture fanatic because she took pictures of all my bruises and scars. I could have even gotten my family members to hurt him, I have some real gangsters in my family but I still loved him. Gangsters meaning we handled business first and ask questions later, that's if you were around to ask questions later. Loving him felt and even sound weird considering all he put me through. How could I love someone who drag me by the hair, punch me in my face with a closed fist, head butt me in the forehead, pull guns on me, encourage me to take drugs, etc. but that's how I felt, there was still a place in my heart for him. He was my daughter father and I did not want to see anything happen to him. The crazy part was he would hurt me at the drop of a hat, but I did not want to see him hurt. During this time there was a woman named Hedda Nussbaum who was a victim of domestic violence. She was beaten so badly by her boyfriend that her whole face was dislocated. This tragic story was all over the news and made major headlines. My friends started calling me Hedda Nussbaum because they saw me in my worse states of abuse. When Hedda Nussbaum face was broadcast on T.V. the world was in shock. She looked horrific. I was in shook that someone would inflict such horrific trauma on someone they loved. But in all actually I was in the same situation. My friends saw me as their Hedda Nussbaum and they wanted to save me. I was upset that they were calling me Her but I was just like her living in fear of my tormentor. I didn't realize the effects the abuse was doing to me until my friends started calling me Hedda. I tried to laugh it off at times but deep down inside it hurt. The reality that I was being beaten to a bloody pulp finally set in. I think you have to look through someone else eyes to see your reality. I was literally beat, battered, abused and I wanted out. I didn't care anymore about the drug money or the amenities that came with this lifestyle. I just wanted to live. I never stopped talking to God. I believed that one day I would be rescued from this life of hell I put myself in. Why did I feel like I put myself in this? Because, when you are a victim of domestic violence you began to blame yourself. You began to ask yourself what can I do differently that will stop him from beating me. In reality it's not the victim that is at fault but the abuser. Yes, I agree that the victim should leave if given the chance, because it never stops at one hit, but the fear that sets in once that first slap, punch, hit or kick is experienced automatically sets in. I never imagines I would be the victim of domestic violence. Growing up I was the type who didn't take any mess from anyone. But, now I know all that I have been through is for a time as today. I pray that my testimony can help someone who may be going through what I have experienced.

Chapter 37

A Change is Gonna Come

I will never forget the day my life changed. The day God answered my prayer. The day I was set free. I will never forget that day the phone came from the 77th precinct. Back in the days when someone was arrested the precinct would call and verify if the person lived at the address they gave upon being arrested. Early that morning the phone rang, I already felt in my heart that something wasn't right because when I woke up in the middle of the night he wasn't home. This was not like him he never slept out. That was one good thing about him he always came home unless he was dealing drugs all night but most of the time he came home. When the phone rang I got a feeling in my gut that something was wrong. The officer on the other line asked me to verify if he lived at this address, his date of birth and phone number. Initially I was shocked that he got arrested again. I automatically knew it was drug related which I knew he would get bailed out. That was the cycle of his life, get arrested, get bailed out, get arrested again, get bailed out again. After the reality set in that I would have a few days of peace, which that's how long it took to see the judge, then I was happy he was arrested and I truly didn't care why. After verifying the information I asked the officer what was the charge and they wouldn't tell me over the phone, but that was ok with me as long it brought me some time to have peace. I remember his mother called me and I told her he was arrested again. A few friends called the house, I had the pleasure of telling everyone who called that he was locked up. He called two days later and said he was going to court the next day so if course I went to court for him. As I was sitting in the courtroom a court appointed lawyer asked was there any family members in the room for him. I stood up and went into the hallway with the lawyer. He told me he was being charged with gang assault. I was in shock. I knew he had a history of putting his hands on people but with a group beating up someone was news to me. When he went before the judge he was declared a Menace to Society and held without bail pending his next court case. I never heard of a person being declared a threat to the world back in this days. That tells you the seriousness of his charges. Look at God working on my behalf the Judge didn't give him a bail. I could not believe he was being held without bail. I could have shouted for joy knowing he didn't even have a chance to get out. No amount of money could have gotten him out of jail. He had a variety of charges, the District Attorney felt he was a flight risk since he wasn't from this country so they held him without bail. That night I went and hung out with my friends and we had a celebration. His next court of about 30 days away so I had thirty days of peace. The next day one of my friends came over to the house, I figured since he was locked already we should called 577-TIPS and tell them about the guns and drugs in the house so they can raid the house an add more charges to his time. I swear to you I sat on the stoop waiting for them to come and raid my house but they never came that day. I figured they would come the next day again they never came. I didn't know what to do next. I was afraid knowing he had the gun, money and drugs in the house. I didn't want any of his friends to come looking for the stash and try to hurt me. The drug game was dangerous and ruthless everyone was out for themselves. I didn't feel safe in the house alone. I didn't know if or when he was coming out of jail. I was too afraid to take his stuff out of the house. I thought let me just stick it out until his next court date and see what happens. The peace and freedom I had was unexplainable. I felt like I was liberated. I was able to sleep at night for the first time in years. I didn't have to worry about him waking up to have sex or slapping me because I snored to loud. When he went back to court they still held him pending his next court date. Now I was really feeling myself he still had to sit in jail for another 45 days. I would go visit him and put his money in his commissary. I told him I wasn't comfortable with the guns and drugs in the house so he told his friend to come and get the stuff. I was happy to be rid of that stuff out of the house. I felt much safer. His friend sold the drugs and gave me the money to give to him. He told me to pay the rent and hold some money because he didn't know how long he would be in there. I couldn't believe my luck. I was so happy truly happy. One day I was in the bathroom about to pray and I looked in the mirror, now I didn't have to pray in the bathroom anymore since he wasn't home but I had gotten so use to it and I felt my prayers were being answered so I decided to keep praying in the bathroom. As I was looking in the mirror which let me just say, I had stopped admiring myself in the mirror because I hated what I would see now, my color was back in my face before I was pale and flushed. I even noticed put on some weight. I could not stop smiling and admiring myself in the mirror. I was a new person after being away from him for this two months. I wasn't worried or scared to go home. I went home to an empty peaceful home no stress, no beatings, no blood droplets to clean up from being beat and bloody. My family and friends were happy to have the old Vanessa back. My job was thriving, I was looking good and feeling good and it showed. I had my glow back walking with my head held. I would go visit my daughter at his mom house but I didn't like going over there anymore because they started acting funny. I wasn't the one who told him to go out there and almost beat someone to death. I was determined to push even harder to get my kids back so I wouldn't have to go back to his mom house to see my daughter. One day my case worker said she wanted to come talk to me but I was at work. She came to my job and told me she wanted to put me in this outpatient program so when I go to court for the kids the judge will see that I am in compliance with the court to have the kids returned to me. She said it is good that I am working but they want to be sure I don't relapse once I got my kids back. She referred me too Kings County Hospital Poly drug Program. I would go there for meeting several days a week after work. It was perfect because I could work and go to the program. I eventually graduated from the program and was given a certificate. My social worker was so impressed with me that she told me she wanted me to take parenting skill classes. These are the things you need to do when you are in the process of having your children returned to you. The good thing was about him being jail was that I could focus on doing everything I needed to do get my kids back. I think he was I didn't have them and his mother had my daughter that way I was under their control. Well that was about to change. I had a reason to live now a fresh start and I was going to take advantage of it. I signed up with this program called Family Dynamics located in the Restoration on Fulton Street in Brooklyn. I was assigned a case worker. I knew I was blessed with him the first day I met him. He was so jovial and seemed to be a nice man. My first appointment we talked for hours. I was totally honest with him about everything. It felt so good to talk to someone who was there just to listen. He didn't judge me he didn't look down on me he just let me empty out. I was crying and he was so comforting me without touching me just a listening ear. He promised me if I did what I needed to do he would sure I got my kids back and my own apartment. I couldn't believe my own apartment. I never had my own apartment. I went from my mom to my daughter father but never my own. So now I had to pull out all stop signs and excel forward. I made a decision I need to move from where we were living to my own place so when he came out I wouldn't have to be in a relationship with him anymore. I truly felt like I could move on. These couple of months away from him gave me the willpower to do what I needed to do for myself. I decided after the next court date I would make my move. I didn't tell anyone about my plans but my mom and new social worker, which they both were in total agreement with my decision.

Chapter 38

Freedom Peace and Liberation

I went to court for him and they still held him without bail. I decided I would stop paying the rent and save my money to move. Eventually, he took a plea deal and was sentenced to 3 years for his crimes. The moment he was sentenced I moved my stuff out of the apartment. I stayed with my mom until eventually I found a kitchenette on Macon street. My first place to call my own, my own keys, my own lease. I did not take anything from the apartment which was everything. I did not want him coming after me if he happened to come out before his time. I had the fear that if I took anything except my clothes he would hunt me down. I called his mom and told her she could pick up the keys from my mother house and I had moved all my stuff out. I didn't have much but my clothes, I was happy with just getting away with my life. His mother wasn't very happy when I told her I moved out. She always felt that we should work our problems out, but I knew she would not have seen it that way if I was her daughter and he was beating me. If the shoe was on the other foot she would have told her daughter to leave him. Some mothers have double standards when it comes to their sons and as much as I loved her she was one of them mothers. Finally, after years of so much bondage and depression I was able to breathe a breath of fresh air. I went full speed ahead in all I needed to do to pick myself up out of the dump he had me in. I was still working at The Board Of Education thank God for that. I decided to go back to school and get my GED. I was determined to get my kids back from my mother who had my son and his mother who had my daughter. I was determined to no longer be a victim to another man's physical abuse. I would either kill him or vice versa but that's how I was thinking from that point on. I finally had some back bone a leg to stand on. I was ready to roar like a lion. I decided I was ready to date other again. I was still afraid of what would happen when he came out of jail. It was a chance I just had to take. I did decide I would inform anyone I dated about him. They needed to know what type of lunatic they would have to deal with in the event he came looking for me. I did not want to put anyone in danger I had enough of him hurting people I loved. I remember one time he was beating on me in my brother house and my uncle, brother, cousin and myself decided to jump him. We were all throwing punches beating the crap out of him or so we through. As we were fighting he comes crawling from under the bottom of the brawl. We were actually fighting and punching each other. When I think about it now it is funny but back then it wasn't. I started going out to all the Clubs celebrating my freedom. My friends were happy for me, my family was happy for me, I was finally free. I stopped going to see him while he was locked up because I knew he was mad about me leaving him. There were no cell phones then only beepers so he could not contact me from jail. I didn't have any communication with him and I loved it. When I did call his mom house to speak to my daughter, his family would tell me he wanted me to come wait for his phone call. That was a joke I wasn't afraid or being controlled by him anymore. Then his mother told me he was being sent upstate to do his time. I was so happy I could have peed on myself. I knew once he went upstate he was going to do all his time. He might get out a few months early for good behavior but he would be gone for at least 2 years. Right after he was sent upstate I went to his mom house to see my daughter. It felt good going over there knowing he wasn't chasing me or coming to beat me up. I think his family was even at ease with all the tension he cause tension gone. I started going to see my daughter more often. She was walking and talking now and I enjoyed watching these moments with her. I would even spend the night over there from time to time. I knew I needed to build these bonding moments with my daughter so when I took back custody of her she would be familiar with me as her mom.

Chapter 39

The Final Straw

One day I was at their house visiting my daughter and his mother asked me to take his sister upstate to see him. His sister had never been to a jail before and did not know much about going to visit him. I didn't want to go because I wasn't too keen on seeing him but I was trying to be nice so I told his mom I would take her up to see him. I had never been upstate to visit anyone in jail before so this would be my first experience as well. I had been to Riker's Island and Brooklyn House of Detention but I had never been to any upstate jails before. We had to be in Manhattan at 12 midnight to catch the bus. The ride upstate was an 8 hour ride on a Greyhound like bus. It was in the middle of winter and was freezing cold outside. His mom paid our bus fare which I think was 40 dollars each plus she gave us spending money for food. The bus ride was long but I kept falling in and out of sleep since it was an overnight trip. We arrived the next morning about 8am and had to be searched. First we went through the metal detector, we had to take off our shoes and empty our pockets. Then we had to put ore bags on a conveyer belt to be searched. They opened your bags and did a thorough search I guess looking for drugs. After being searched we put our stuff in lockers. We then had to wait for our names to be called. We were taken from one waiting room into another just to sit some more. Finally they called his name and we stood up. The officer took us to a large room which seemed to have a hundred tables in it. All the tables were nailed to the floor but you could move the chairs. The officer sat us down and said he would be right out. I was a little nervous about seeing him. I had not seen him in about 6 months. I made sure I was looking hot. I had my hair freshly done and I had on a new outfit and new shoes. I wanted him to see the new and improved me. No longer the beat battered and abused me but the strong independent and high self -esteem me. When he came out from behind the big steel door I must admit he looked handsome. He had put on some weight I guess he was working out in jail. Jail always bring out the physical fitness in a man. I guess that's all they have to do is lift weights and his showed. We got some snacks out the vending machine for us to eat. He got a deck of cards off the game rack they had with different board games and cards. He and his sister did most of the talking. I sat there looking around at other people on their visits. I could tell he was upset with me because he wasn't saying much. I didn't care though because his mother asked me to bring his sister not for him. We had been on the visit for about an hour when he finally started talking to me. He wasn't really talking to me but rather asking me questions. More like talking at me interrogating. Why did I move out of the apartment? Why did I leave his stuff in the apartment? What happened to his money and stuff that was in the speaker he kept as his stash? I was getting snotty with him because I felt he had no business asking me anything that was 6 months ago, furthermore I felt like I was no longer In fear of him so I didn't have to bite my tongue anymore. I had to remind him that the money I was putting in his commissary was his drug money that he told his friend to take the drugs and sell. I also told him in a not so nice tone of voice didn't I have to pay the rent and your bills just in case he came home didn't you need a place to live. He was giving me the dirtiest look but I didn't care. What could he do to me he was incarcerated and I was free so I felt he couldn't hurt me anymore. To break the tension his sister suggested we take a picture. I didn't mind after all I looked cute. There was an inmate who took pictures so we signed up to take pictures. After we went to the front and paid we had to wait for them to call us up to take our picture. That went ok pictures taken and we were now back at our table. He started up with me again and started calling me all kinds of names talking about I stole his money. I told him I didn't steal your money how much did you think you had left after I paid your rent. Well, I guess he got pissed off with me for my snotty answers and his old self kicked in. He must have forgot where he was because one minute we were arguing about how I just left his stuff in the house and what happened to his money and drugs. Well, before

I knew it he slapped me so hard in my face that my head did a 360 degree turn on my shoulders. If I wasn't sitting in the chair I'm sure the impact of the hit I would have ended up on the floor. That is how hard he slapped me. Thank God he hit me with an open hand and not his fist. The force would have probably knocked out my teeth. The crazy things was I saw when he pulled his hand back I was use to how he would position his hand before he would hit me. I didn't think he was going to hit me especially in the visiting room of a jail way upstate New York. But then I had to remember who I was dealing with. A man who had no respect for authority, who didn't care about his own life so I knew he didn't care about mines. As I composed myself from the shock of being hit, before I knew it there came running 3 huge redneck State Correction officers. They literally picked my daughter father up off his feet and carried him out of the visiting area. Two of them had him by the arms and one of them had him in a headlock arms wrapped around his neck. I thought they were going to break his neck. His sister is now crying I guess from watching them manhandled him. Several more officers came rushed us out of the visiting room. They made everyone stay in their seats the inmates and the visitors. Everyone was looking at me, I was more embarrassed than anything. I wasn't even crying, see they didn't know I was use to this abuse so I couldn't cry anymore. I was numb at this point nothing he did could hurt me. Since being away from him I developed a strength I didn't even know I had so I couldn't cry. The officers made me and his sister leave the visiting and go back into   back into the main waiting room. The Captain and Head of the Prison, the white shirts came out to talk to me about what happened. I explained everything to them about what happened and why I was there in the first place which was basically just to bring his sister up there. They tried to convince me to press charges against him I thought about it. The Captain told me I would have to come up there to the court and testify because it was an assault. I told them I could not come all the way back up there just for a court date. They explained to me rather I testified or not he was going to get more time for assaulting me on the jail property but I he could also face additional charges for assaulting me. I expressed my fear of him knowing when he got out he would come after me. I didn't want to be the cause of him getting more time. They were looking at me like I was out of my mind but no one knew the fear this man had instilled in me of him. I wasn't afraid as long as I knew he couldn't get to me but what about when he was released who would protect me then. I would be looking over my shoulder for the rest of my life. After they took my statement and his sister statement which she was reluctant to give one but because she was there when it happened she had to write as well. I asked them if it was possible that his sister could go back on the visit because I was only there to bring her up there. I did not want to go back on the visit but I literally begged them to allow her just a little more time with him. There was still about 5 hours left on the visit. Originally they could not allow the visit to continue and we were both crying now. The Captain said they needed to have a discussion. So they left and we sat there not really saying anything to each other. I felt she was upset with me for what happened like it was my fault that he hit me. But again they always felt like it was my fault when he assaulted me anyway. Not even considering her brother just slapped fire out of me in front of hundreds of people. It was like she forgot we were on a jail visit and not in their living room where he has beat me before or the fact that I have to get back on the bus with some of those same people. About an hour passed and finally the captain came out with an officer and said they would allow her to go back on the visit but I couldn't go. I reiterated to them that I never wanted to see his face ever again but I was so grateful they would allow her to go back on the visit with him. They took her back inside for the last few hours of the visit. I took my coat out the locker, laid across the bench and went to sleep. I was tired anyway from the cold, uncomfortable, long bus ride. I was glad to stretch out across the bench and take a nap. I knew I could get a few hours of sleep so I got comfortable. I was the only one in the waiting room besides and officer stationed at the desk. I didn't realize how long I had been sleeping until she woke me up when the visit was over. We got our stuff out of the locker to board the bus really not saying much to each other. Once on the bus I wasn't sleepy, I had slept on the bench. I looked out the window most of the ride home. I was disgusted with her attitude so I ignored her the whole ride home. I made a decision right then and there that I was never ever going to see or speak to him again if I could help it. I know we share a daughter but I felt he could have a relationship with her through his mother not me. I would never deny him the opportunity to see his daughter but I didn't want any parts of him.

Chapter 40

God Answered My Prayer

He spent 3 years upstate in jail. During the time of his incarceration I attained my General Equivalent Diploma (GED), finished a drug treatment program which was a requirement to have my son and daughter returned back to my custody and moved into my own apartment. I remember his mother called me one day so distraught. He was due for release from jail in a couple of months and the courts decided to deport him back to his place of birth Barbados. The courts declared him a Menace to Society and ordered him to be deported straight after the completion of his time in prison. It was a bitter sweet moment for me to be honest. I knew how much he loved my daughter his only child and the fact that he had missed so much of her early years, also his mom loved him so much and now he had to be deported straight from jail. The happy part was I did not have to see him anytime soon. But wait, it hit me one day that this God whom I was not even fully serving, this God whom I prayed to but didn't have an intimate relationship with, This God whom I didn't think even heard my prayers or knew who I was, this God who I never seen but I did believe he existed, this God who only hear from me when I need him, this God whom I didn't even go to church and pray to, this God whom I didn't open the Bible and read his word, ANSWERED MY PRAYER. I prayed and asked God hundreds of times "don't hurt him, don't kill him, but just take him out of my life". Now here we are years later and it has finally happened. He spent three years in prison and upon his release he is being deported. Only

God!! I didn't know much about people being deported so I asked my friends from the islands. They explained to me when a person is deported they are not allowed back into the country they were deported from. This being the United States of America he could not come back here. The only way he could come back is if he sneak back or he would have to go to the highest Courts or the United States Embassy and ask, but once a person have all the drug and assault charges he have it is very unlikely they would allow him to come back into the country. I didn't even realize that my prayer was answered until I got the call that he was being deported. Me, this sinner, Drinking, Drugging, getting high, cursing , fighting, fornicating, selling drugs, stabbed somebody, bust somebody in the head with a chair, and God still answered my prayers. I will never forget my prayer "God don't hurt him, don't kill him, just take him out of my life" look at God "He's not hurt, He's not dead, but he is out of my life". Glory Hallelujah. Hallelujah is the highest praise. I never thought I was worthy of God's love. I mean, were talking about the Almighty Creator of the Universe Heaven and the Earth. He spoke and there was light. He spoke and the earth was formed. He made man from dust. He made woman from man's rib. He parted the Red Sea. He raised the dead. Wow how amazing to have this God who loves me in spite of me. In spite of my messy disorganized life. I never really knew how to pray but I knew I could talk to God and he will hear me. I grew up in church as a child. They kept us in church, Sunday school, Bible Study, Youth Service, Children's Choir, Youth Choir you name it we did it. Then I went deep into the world, as I got older I wanted to be grown and live my own life, so I thought. I have now given my life to Christ. Through many hard trials and hundreds of obstacles. Through brokenness mentally, physically and emotionally, I decided I didn't want control of my life anymore. I just made bad decision after bad decision. I was ready to surrender and submit my life to Christ. Five Baptisms later and a host of churches under my belt, I have finally come to understand what the true meaning of being a Christian is. Being a Christian is not about a religion but about a relationship with Christ. People can change their religion in fact there are so many religions that a person can pick and choose which one they want to be. However, a relationship with God/Jesus Christ is a lifelong decision a life changing decision. A relationship with Christ will benefit your life. Your life will forever be changed for the better. You will walk different, talk different, see things different, change your way of thinking, your life will be blessed abundantly I am a living testimony to the goodness of God. His Grace his mercy. Grace is the unmerited favor of God over our lives that we don't deserve, we have all fallen short of the Glory of God but yet he still gives us Grace. Mercy is what God have for us even in our sin he is merciful. Mercy is God not giving us what we deserve. We are again all sinners saved by the Grace and Mercy of God. The funny thing about giving my life to Christ is that it was not my choice. I would be lying if I said I made a decision to change. I enjoyed living in the world being. I enjoyed being the social butterfly of the party. I enjoyed being miss popularity. Everyone Knew "RED" which was my nick name giving to me by the hood. I loved dropping it like it's hot in the clubs, gyrating my hips in a sexually explicit way, making all the men drool and lust after me. I loved being known as a dance hall queen in the reggae clubs. I loved being known as a no nonsense chick who would bust anybody including your momma upside the head. I loved smoking weed, smoking cigarettes, drinking alcohol, having boyfriends who took care of me and paid my bills. Hell, I even liked the domestic violence sometimes because I felt like he loved me that's why he beat me. I always got money and nice things after the beatings well most of the time that was his way of making up to me. I loved the fact that my house was the hang out house, the place to be. Card games, drinking and smoking weed parties, social gatherings, I loved this life. I thought I was living not realizing I was just existing. Today I am living with a purpose my life has meaning. Since giving my life to Christ I have become a new person. Well, truthfully speaking I cannot take any credit for my change. I was still running the other way as God was pulling me towards salvation. I knew my family wouldn't understand, my friends wouldn't accept the new and improved me, my man wouldn't understand the change I made. I was afraid of losing all I had known and was use to 'The World'. Since Christ took over my life I have become a new person. I now know I have a purpose for living. That purpose is to see the Kingdom of Heaven when I am called home. That purpose is to touch as many lives as I can along the way. That purpose is to introduce people to the salvation of the Lord. To use my testimony to help other sufferers of Molestation, Domestic violence and Drug abuse. I also want as many lives to get to the kingdom of Heaven as well. God gave us two arms for a reason, one to reach for the stars the other to pull someone up along the way with you. To reach your highest potential you have to look to God he holds the keys to your future. I have been through so much in my life that I've seen the good side of life, the bad side of life and the ugly side of life. I can say since I came to know Jesus my life has been so much better. I see the light at the end of the tunnel. Now don't get it twisted it wasn't easy being me. I can honestly say there were many times when I didn't even like myself. Nothing in life was handed to me, it was through blood, sweat and tears that I am where I am today. I had to endure so much heartache through my growing pains. God gave me the strength to tell my story or rather my testimony, believe me I had rather not tell my business to the world, but when God tell you to move you better move. I remember when the idea first came to write a book about what I been through in the early years of my life. I was torn even ashamed about putting my life experiences on paper for the world to read. God showed me, I am not defined by my past but what Christ have for my future. There was a time I would have never talked about my past, let alone wrote a book. When God told me he would use my testimony to help others, I figured there is nothing to be ashamed about. I started thinking how will they know my testimony if I don't tell it. I had to learn my past is what shaped my future. I have learned so much about me, about life, about hurt, and about pain that I could spend a lifetime sharing my story. I have so much more to tell but I decided to save it for another book. AMEN TO GOD BE THE GLORY FOR THE COMPLETION OF BOOK 1.

THANK YOU JESUS FOR YOUR PRECIOUS BLOOD THAT WAS SHED FOR THE REMISSION OFMY SINS, FOR YOUR LOVE, FOR YOUR GRACE, FOR YOUR MERCY, FOR YOUR PEACE, FOR YOUR JOY, FOR YOUR STRENGTH, FOR YOUR PROVISIONS, FOR YOUR DIVINE INTEREVENTION, FOR YOUR PROTECTION AND FOR THIS BOOK. WITHOUT YOU NOTHING IS POSSIBLE. I AM NOTHING WITHOUT YOU. GLORY HALLELJUAH TO YOUR PRECIOUS NAME. YOU LORD DESERVE ALL THE HONOR GLORY AND PRAISE. IN YOUR PRECIOUS NAME I PRAY, AMEN, AMEN AND AMEN.

LET THE WORDS OF MY MOUTH AND THE MEDITATION OF MY HEART BE ACCEPTABLE IN THY SIGHT FOR YOU ALONE LORD ARE MY STRENGTH AND MY REDEEMER.